THE STROUD
VALLEY
ILLVSTRATED

THE STROUD VALLEY

ILLVSTRATED

New edition 2008

The History Press Ltd
The Mill, Brimscombe Port
Stroud, Gloucestershire, GL5 2QG
www.thehistorypress.co.uk

British Library Cataloguing in Publication Data.
A catalogue record for this book is available from the British Library.

ISBN 978 0 7524 4817 6

Typesetting and origination by The History Press Ltd.
Printed in Great Britain

PUBLISHER'S NOTE: NEW EDITION

Stroud has witnessed many changes since the original version of this book was first published over 100 years ago. A fourth reprint, from 1911, was recently discovered in a local resident's collection, and contains many of the advertisements and photographs that were created at the time, giving the modern reader a glimpse into Stroud Valley life all those decades ago. The original edition of this book was published in the late nineteenth century by 'Burrow's Royal Series', and is therefore in demand by antiquarian book dealers and collectors.

Looking at the shop fronts as they were, local residents can recognise the shops they know today, and perhaps even uncover some of the history of their own shops, while noticing the buildings and interiors that have changed relatively little since the first years of the twentieth century.

The images of Stroud's landscape are particularly interesting, revealing how the development and modernisation of the town has altered life for residents. How Stroud and its environs were perceived before the First World War is very different from the modern outlook of a busy, thriving town. Residents of Amberley, Birdlip, Minchinhampton, Nailsworth, Painswick, Rodborough, Selsley and Slad will also find this book of immense interest, as it includes information on these locations which have been influenced by the changes that have taken place in Stroud over the years.

George Redman & Son, the tailors and outfitters located at 27 George Street in Stroud, may have long since gone, but who lives there or has a business there now? We all recognise the breathtaking view from Selsley Hill but, looking at it as it was in the Victorian era on page 81, we can see how Stroud has developed and expanded, influencing the local communities. Does anyone recognise the black and white photograph of Stroud Post Office? Perhaps someone reading this now owns the building and can provide yet more information. Reading through this guide, one almost feels as though they are stepping back in time and could walk right into Hobbs Confectionary on George Street to buy one of their cakes.

This valuable historical guide contains a cornucopia of photographs, advertisements and information relating to Stroud and its neighbouring villages and towns. As well as general information, the book includes interesting chapters on drives and short cycle trips, a list of flowering plants in Gloucestershire, the geology of mid-Gloucestershire, archaeological notes on the district, and church bells of mid-Gloucestershire.

You can read this book from the comfort of your armchair or, perhaps more adventurously, while walking around the shops and streets featured, noting the changes and the buildings which locals recognise so well, yet may know little about. It is certainly a nostalgic read for those who have lived in the area for many years and members of local historical societies, and a fascinating insight for those visiting or new to the Five Valleys.

R. E. COX, ❧

Ladies' and
Gentlemen's Tailor.

Department for ❧ Hosiery,   Ties,   Gloves,
                 Shirts,   Braces,   Hats,
                 Collars,   Scarves,   Umbrellas.

3, GEORGE STREET, STROUD.

W. H. GILLMAN, &

Hosier, Hatter, Glover, Shirt and Collar Maker.

Agent for Lincoln, Bennett & Co.'s Hats,

The Celebrated Aertex Cellular Clothing.

SPÉCIALITÉ:

SAMPLE SHIRTS TO MEASURE IN 48 HOURS.

FIT GUARANTEED.

YOUR KIND PATRONAGE RESPECTFULLY SOLICITED.

ECONOMY IN COALS!

Buy from...

Dickinson, Prosser & Cox,

RUSSELL STREET, STROUD;
(Next door to General Post Office)

CHALFORD: Agent, G. H. MANN;
WOODCHESTER: Agent, A. VIRGO;

whose Qualities recommend themselves
with One Trial.

Now supplying Truck Loads direct to most Counties in England.

WHOLESALE OR RETAIL LISTS ON APPLICATION.

King Street Mediæval Iron Works
STROUD.

T. L. CHEW & SONS,

Manufacturers of Wrought-Iron Gates, Fencing, Railings, Ornamental Ironwork, Casements, Hinges, and every description of Ironwork for Church and other purposes.

General and Furnishing Ironmongers.

Electric and Crank Bell Hangers, Gas, Steam and Hot=Water Fitters, and General Smiths.

Agents for the best Makers of...

Agricultural and Horticultural Implements.

Stroud Sanitary Laundry Co., Ltd.,

EBLEY, near Stroud, Glos.

This Laundry, being under the Factory Act, PERFECT SANITATION is Guaranteed.

No Work of an Undesirable Kind Received.

Special Terms for Schools, Houses of Business, Hotels and Public Institutions.

NO CHEMICALS INJURIOUS TO LINEN USED.

The Company's Vans Call for and Deliver Work.

Price List on Application.

All Communications respecting work, etc., to be addressed to "The Manageress."

TERMS: - CASH ON DELIVERY.

16

WITHEY & WITHEY,

. . Wine Merchants,

STROUD.

Scotch Whisky:

			Per doz.	Per bot.
Choice Old Beverton	=	=	42/=	3/6
(See Analytical Report).				
Special Reserve ditto	=	=	48/=	4/=
Withey's Blend	=	=	42/=	3/6
(Very Fine).				
Withey's Pure Highland Malt			42/=	3/6

Vintages Ports:

**Bottled by WITHEY & WITHEY,
and Shipped by
COCKBURN, SANDEMAN, MARTINEZ,
and other First=class Shippers.**

1875	......	Bottled	......	1878	
1878	......	,,	......	1881	
1881	......	,,	......	1884	
1884	......	,,	......	1887	
1887	......	,,	......	1890	Prices on application.
1890	......	,,	......	1893	
1896	......	,,	......	1899	

These Wines, not having been moved since Bottling,
are in perfect condition.

WITHEY & WITHEY,
Wine Merchants, Stroud.

Established 1806.

A. G. Tyler

Wholesale . .

Cabinet Manufacturer,

.. BRIMSCOMBE.

Offices and Showrooms:
Brimscombe Cabinet Works.

Telegrams: "Tyler, Brimscombe."
Telephone 1 X 2.   ,,

Showrooms at **48, High Street, Stroud;**
and **20a, Working Street, Cardiff.**

National Telephone: 01221.

SPECIALITIES:—

Bedroom Suites, Sideboards,
Dining and Drawing Room Suites.

. . . All in the Latest Designs.

Catalogues, Special Designs and Estimates on application.

J. & J. Cetta

Jewellers and Cutlers.

Watches, Clocks, Jewellery,
Electro-plated Goods in great variety.   Wholesale and Retail.

Barometers, Thermometers and Jewellery Repaired.

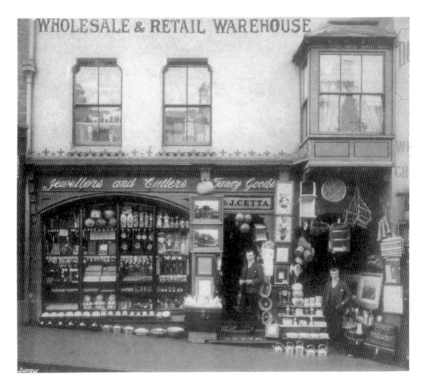

The Noted Shop for Wedding, Fancy and Keeper Rings.

A Good Assortment of Fancy Goods   Knives and Forks, Carvers, &c.
of every description.   Glass and China Goods.

A Nice Assortment of Dinner and Tea Services.

Established 1833.   **High Street, STROUD.**

22

S. M. STRANGE,

Wholesale and Family Grocer,

19, King Street, STROUD.

Nat. Telephone 0294.

SPECIALITIES. ✢ ✢ ✢

Choice Teas and Coffees, - - -
High-Class Groceries and Provisions,
English and Foreign Fruits, - -
Californian Dried Fruits. - - -

Attention is drawn to the illustration, representing a fine consignment of BANANAS, from Kingston, Jamaica. This splendid fruit arrives fortnightly by the Imperial Direct West India Mail Service.

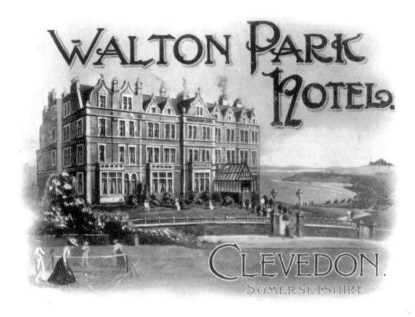

PHILIP FORD & SON,

**Builders, Undertakers,
Shop Fitters,**

Slad Road, STROUD.

Interior of Carpenters' Shop.

Contractors to His Majesty's Government.

FUNERALS PERSONALLY CONDUCTED.

TELEPHONE 142Y1.

Burrow's 'Royal' Official

ABERDEEN.—The Grand Hotel.
Quiet, Comfortable, First-class Hotel. Excellent Cuisine. Hotel Porter meets all Trains. Tariff, with Views of the City and Neighbourhood, sent on application.

ABERGAVENNY.—Angel Hotel. John Prichard, Proprietor.
Fishing, Golf, Mountain Scenery.

ABERYSTWITH.—Queen's Hotel.

BATH.—Empire Hotel.
Finest Hotel in the West of England. Close to the Abbey, Baths and Pump Room. Carefully Heated and Ventilated. Orchestra. Excellent Cuisine.

BEN RHYDDING, YORKSHIRE.—Hydro Hotel.
80 acres of Pleasure Grounds. Magnificent Scenery. Bracing Air. Private Golf Course of 9 Sporting Holes. Telegrams—"Hydro, Ben Rhydding."

BEXHILL.—Sackville Hotel. Proprietors: The Frederick Hotels, Limited.
Finest Position. Facing Sea. Close to Kursaal. The only Hotel on the De La Warr Estate.

BIRMINGHAM.—Great Western Hotel, Colmore Row. T. W. Hussey, Manager.
Table d'Hôte. Night Porter. Telegraphic Address—"Hostelry." Telephone 929.

BIRMINGHAM.—Queen's Hotel.
Under the management of the L. & N. W. Railway Company. Lighted throughout by Electricity. Telephone No. 496. Telegraphic Address - "Northwestern Hotel, Birmingham."

BOURNEMOUTH.—Hotel Metropole. W. E. Odlum, Manager.
"A palace amidst the pines in a flood of sunshine." 200 Rooms. Facing South. Lifts to all Floors. Electric Light. Illustrated Tariff and Terms from Manager.

BRECON.—Castle Hotel.
Fishing, Mountain Scenery. Old-established and Comfortable.

BRISTOL.—Royal Hotel, College Green. Helen Rogers, Manageress.
First-class Family and Commercial. Electric Elevator. Telephone 491. Telegraphic Address—"Banquet," Bristol. Night Porter. Private Omnibus.

BUSHEY, HERTS.—The Hall. Manager, Colonel Coyne.
16 miles from Euston. First-class Hotel. Country Residence by Day or Week Turkish Baths. Golf Links. Address, Manager.

BUXTON.—Crescent Hotel. C. J. Smilter, Proprietor.
Close to Station; opposite Pumproom. Covered Colonnade to Baths, Wells and Gardens. Excellent Cuisine at inclusive terms. Electric Light.

CAMBRIDGE.—The Bull Hotel.

CARDIFF.—Royal Hotel. H. F. Richardson, Manager.
The most modern and comfortable Hotel in Wales. Central. Electric Light. Lifts. Well-lighted Stockrooms. Bus meets Trains.

CHELTENHAM.—Queen's Hotel.
Most Commodious Hotel in Cheltenham. Facing Promenade and Winter Gardens. Lift to Each Floor. Electric Light. High-class Posting. Special Accommodation for Hunters at Livery.

CHELTENHAM.—Tate's Private Hotel.
Centre of Promenade, near Ladies' College. Most Cheerful, Comfortable and Homelike. Excellent Catering under Personal Management. Terms Moderate and Inclusive.

CHESTER.—Queen Hotel. W. H. Burleigh, Manager.
First-class. Connected with General Railway Station by Covered Way. Porters in Scarlet Livery meet Trains Day and Night. Passenger Lift.

CLEVEDON.—Walton Park Hotel.
Facing the Sea. Amongst Pine Woods. Every Modern Comfort. Sumptuously Furnished. Golf. Tennis. Coaching. Billiards. Send for Booklet. Telegrams—"Parkotel, Clevedon." See Illustrated Advertisement.

CLIFTON.—Cliftondown Hotel.
Unrivalled Scenery. Lowest Death-rate in England. High-class Family Hotel managed by the Proprietor. Telegraphic Address—"Suspension, Bristol." Telephone, 550 Bristol.

DOVER.—Hotel Burlington. Proprietors: The Frederick Hotels, Limited.
Finest Coast Hotel in England. Splendid Position, Centre of Esplanade. Opposite Promenade Pier.

EDINBURGH.—The Palace Hotel. John Ferguson, Proprietor.
Occupying the finest site in Edinburgh. Immediately opposite the Castle and Public Gardens. First-class House. Personal Management.

FLEETWOOD.—North Euston Hotel. Manageress: E. S. Clarkson.
One minute from Station. Promenade Roof. Splendid Sea View. Excellent Cuisine. Electric Light. Fishing. Boating. Telephone, 0198. Tariff, Manageress.

FOLKESTONE.—Royal Pavilion Hotel. Proprietors: The Frederick Hotels, Limited.
Facing the Sea. All Home Comforts. Adjoins Harbour Station for Cross-Channel Service.

FOLKESTONE.—Wampach's Hotel. C. C. Wampach, Managing Director.
First-class. Excellent Cuisine. Moderate Terms en Pension. Passenger Lift. Motor Storage. Omnibus meets all Trains at Central Station.

Burrow's 'Royal' Official Handbooks are also to be seen in

First=Class Hotels.

Handbooks

are to be seen in the Reading Rooms or Lounges of All Hotels in This List, besides many others not detailed here.

GLASGOW.—Central Station Hotel.
Under the management of the Caledonian Railway Company. 400 Rooms. Excellent Accommodation. Inclusive Terms. Table d'Hôte meals a speciality.

HAMPTON COURT, MIDDLESEX.—Mitre Hotel.
Beautifully situated by the River Thames and overlooking the famous Palace. Close to Railway Station. Noted House for Banquets.

HARROGATE.—Hotel Majestic. Proprietors: The Frederick Hotels, Ltd.
Stands in own Grounds, overlooking Pump Room, Municipal Baths and Spa Grounds.

HARROGATE.—North=Eastern Station Hotel.
Immediately Opposite the Station. First-class Family and Commercial Hotel, Restaurant and Stock Rooms. Electric Light. For Tariff apply Manager.

ILFRACOMBE.—Runnacleave Hotel.
South Aspect. 150 Rooms. Large Recreation Hall. Billiards. Skating Rink. Included in Moderate Tariff. Illustrated Booklet on Application.

ILFRACOMBE.—The Ilfracombe Hotel. H. Russell Grover, Manager.
Standing in its own ornamental grounds of 5 acres, contains 250 apartments. On the Seashore. Tariff and lowest inclusive terms of Manager.

ILKLEY.—Craiglands Hydro. Manager, J. Dobson.

KILLARNEY.—Great Southern Hotel.
Under Railway Management. Situated Convenient to Principal Scenery and Railway. Largest and Most Modern in the District. Thirty Acres Ornamental Grounds.

LIMERICK.—Great Southern Hotel, Junction.
Under Railway Management. Convenient when breaking journey on the way to Cork, Waterford, Limerick, etc. Quite Modern. Entrance from Platform.

LIVERPOOL.—Compton Hotel, Church Street. W. Russell, Proprietor.
Occupies the Finest Site in the City, overlooking the Cathedral Gardens. Telegrams —"Compton." Telephones—58, 8058, 0160.

LLANDUDNO.—St. George's Hotel. Thomas P. Davies, Resident Proprietor.
Premier Position. Facing the Sea. Electric Light Throughout. Hydraulic Lift. Table d'Hôte served at Separate Tables. Apply, Proprietor.

LONDON, E.C.—Manchester Hotel, Aldersgate Street.
Family and Commercial Hotel. Centrally Situated. Bed, Breakfast and Attendance, 6/6. Stock Rooms. Electric Light. Lift. Tariff on Application.

LONDON.—Euston Hotel, Euston Station. R. H. Glasspool, Manager.

LONDON.—Hotel Great Central. Proprietors: The Frederick Hotels, Ltd.
Near the Great Western and Great Central Railway Termini. Five minutes' walk from Oxford Street.

LONDON.—Hotel Russell. Proprietors: The Frederick Hotels, Limited.
Close to Great Northern Midland and London & North-Western Termini. Central for West-End and City.

LONDON.—Great Western Royal Hotel, Paddington.
For Families and Gentlemen. Table d'Hôte, Breakfasts and Dinners. Electric Light Throughout. Passenger Lift. Porters meet all Trains.

MARGATE.—Hotel Metropole.
Facing the Jetty. Splendid Sea Views. Magnificently Furnished and Decorated. Elevator. Lounges. Up-to-date. Moderate inclusive charges.

MATLOCK.—Smedley's Hydropathic Establishment. H. Challand, Manager.
Established 1853. One of the largest and most complete in the Kingdom. Illustrated Prospectus on application.

MINEHEAD.—Hotel Metropole.
Facing Sea. Hunting, Fishing and Golf.

STROUD.—Imperial Hotel. Mrs. Lawson, Proprietress.
Every comfort and convenience for visitors. Suites of private rooms. Opposite G.W.R. Station.

STROUD.—Royal George Hotel. R. Callingham, Proprietor.
Family, Commercial and Posting House. Stalls for Hunters. Headquarters C.T.C. and Automobile Club.

TENBY.—Royal Gate House Hotel. Resident Proprietor, F. W. Gregory.
Immediately overlooking Sea. Good Public Rooms. Private Suites. Cuisine. Wines Excellent. Moderate Terms. Golf. Billiards. Good Stabling.

WESTON=SUPER=MARE.—The Grand Atlantic.
The healthiest and most invigorating seaside resort in the world. The GRAND ATLANTIC is the principal Hotel, with every modern convenience and comfort, strictly moderate tariff.—Apply Manager.

WHITBY.—Hotel Metropole. Proprietors: The Frederick Hotels, Limited.
The Leading Hotel in Whitby. Beautifully situated on the Leas. Open during Summer.

WORCESTER.—Star Hotel. G. E. Spur, Proprietor.
The Leading County Family and Commercial Hotel. Electric Light Throughout. Ladies' Drawing Room. Billiard Rooms. Smoking Rooms.

the Saloons of the **Elder Dempster** and other Steamboat lines.

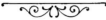

30

Wood & Rowe,

Coal, Salt and Builders' Merchants, Cheapside, **STROUD.**

Best House and **Steam Coals.**

Anthracite and **Coke.**

All kinds of Staffordshire Bricks, Pipes, Cements, Forest Stone, Chimney Pots, etc., etc., in stock. Prices on application.

Head Office:—STROUD. Telephone No. 44.

DEPOTS:—Nailsworth, Ryeford, Stonehouse and Frocester.

G. Sparkes Powell,

Whitehall Bakery, and at 74, Middle Street, **STROUD.**

Baker and Flour Dealer.

Superfine Flour. Self=Raising Flour.

Cakes of all kinds at 4d., 6d. and 8d. per lb.

Your patronage respectfully solicited. A Delivery Daily to all parts of the Town and Neighbourhood.

The Stroud News and Gloucester County Advertiser

THE CONSERVATIVE ORGAN
OF THE MID-GLOUCESTER DIVISION.

ESTABLISHED 1867.

Biggest, Brightest and Best Paper in the District.

Circulates in Five Constituencies

Stroud, Cirencester and Tewkesbury Divisions, and Cheltenham and Gloucester Parliamentary Boroughs.

THE MOST EFFECTIVE ADVERTISING MEDIUM IN MID=GLOUCESTERSHIRE.

Reaches all Classes.   Cheap Scale for Public Wants.

EVERY FRIDAY MORNING—ONE PENNY.

The Best-Equipped General Printing Office
in the Division.

OFFICES :—
GEORGE STREET, STROUD, GLOS.

A. H. Shepherd,

16 & 17, King Street, Stroud.

Court Dressmakers,

Court Milliners.

Wedding Gowns,	**Bridesmaids' Dresses,**
Costumes,	**Millinery,**
Mantles.	**Tea Gowns.**

EXQUISITE ORIGINAL DESIGNS.

RICHEST MATERIALS.   PERFECTION OF FIT.

T. P. Anthony & Co.,

HIGH-CLASS DRAPERS.

SILK MERCERS, LADIES' OUTFITTERS, FURRIERS, Etc.

Showrooms for Mantles.

MILLINERY, ÷ BLOUSES, ÷ UNDERCLOTHING,
÷ ÷ ÷ DRESSMAKING. ÷ ÷ ÷

Funerals Furnished Throughout.

SMITH & Co.,

Dispensing and Family Chemists,
. . Market Place, STROUD.

DEALERS in . .

Photographic Chemicals,
Cameras, Dry Plates, Films,
Printing-Out Papers,
Mounts, Dishes,

and every requisite for the Amateur Photographer.

Special attention given to the...

DEVELOPING & PRINTING of AMATEURS' NEGATIVES.

SPECIALITIES.

Smith's Combined Toning and Fixing Solution.

Smith's Pyro=Soda Developer.

Smith's Special Film Developer. Strongly recommended for Kodak Films.

Smith's One=Solution Developer. For Snap-shots, Velox, Dekko and Bromide Papers.

Dark=Room Free to Customers.

Telephone No. 79.

SMITH'S GUINEA HAND CAMERA.

36

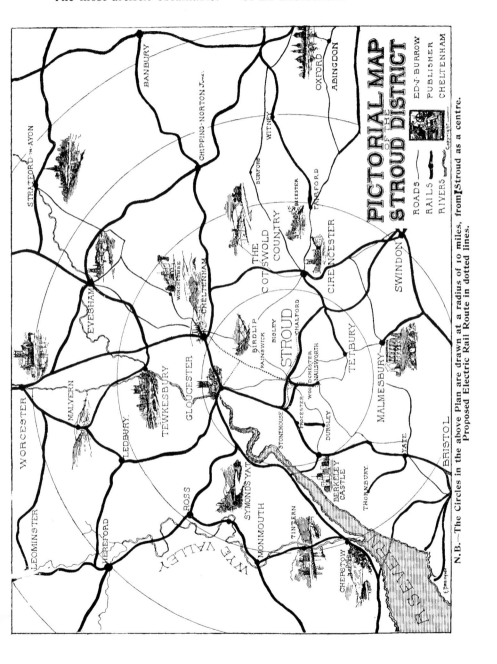

PICTORIAL MAP OF THE STROUD DISTRICT

ED·J·BURROW
PUBLISHER
CHELTENHAM

ROADS
RAILS
RIVERS

N.B.—The Circles in the above Plan are drawn at a radius of 10 miles, from Stroud as a centre. Proposed Electric Rail Route in dotted lines.

37

STREET MAP OF STROUD.

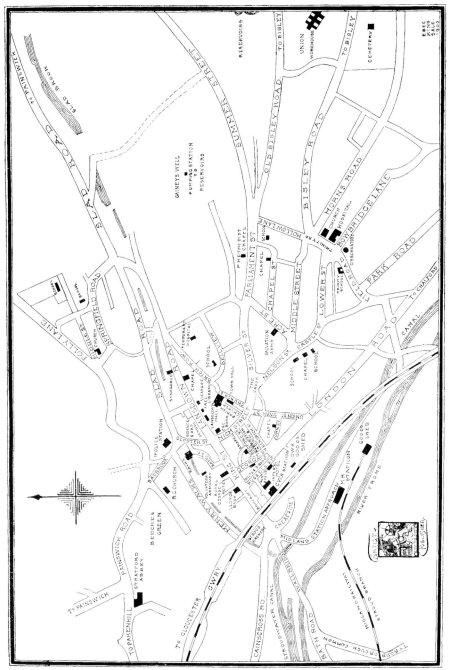

Compiled by Mr. S. G. Cull, of , specially for this publication.　　　　COPYRIGHT.

Browning

BUTCHER and PURVEYOR
of High-class Home-killed Meat only.

PRIMEST SCOTCH and DEVON BEEF.

COTSWOLD, DOWN and WELSH MUTTON.

CHOICEST VEAL, LAMB and DAIRY-FED PORK.

SPECIALITIES:
Sweetbreads,
Pickled Ox Tongues,
Corned Beef.

Daily District Delivery.

SPECIAL TERMS:
for Hotels,
Boarding Houses,
and other large
Establishments.

PATRONAGE RESPECTFULLY SOLICITED.

The ONLY Address: **Cotswold House, 17, Gloucester St., STROUD.**

Established over Half a Century.

TELEPHONE No. 0280.

SECOND EDITION.

THE STROUD VALLEY

ILLUSTRATED

INCLUDING NAILSWORTH, PAINSWICK, CHALFORD AND EBLEY.

(Issued under the combined Auspices of the Stroud Urban District Council and the Stroud and District Traders' Association.)

WITH SPECIALLY-WRITTEN ARTICLES

BY

THE REV. E. HAWKINS, M.A.	S. J. COLEY.
THE REV. C. A. DAVIS.	JAS. HARPER, ⎫ Ebley.
MRS. JOHN WHITE.	J. R. PEARSON, ⎭
MISS E. P. FENNIMORE.	C. W. JONES, Nailsworth,
W. THOMPSON.	and
CHAS. UPTON.	GEO. HOLMES.

EDITED BY MR. W. THOMPSON,
Of the "Stroud Journal."

Price 6d.

Printed and Published by

EDWARD J. BURROW, ART PUBLISHER. CHELTENHAM;

AND 3, AMEN CORNER, LONDON.

—— *Printed at The Country Press, Bradford.*

Central Photographic

Stores,

CAMERAS AND APPARATUS.
PLATES AND PAPERS.

AN ABUNDANT AND FRESH SUPPLY OF ALL THE
BEST-KNOWN MAKES KEPT IN STOCK.

DEVELOPING AND PRINTING FOR AMATEURS.

Best Workmanship.

ROLL FILMS A SPECIALITY.

S. J. COLEY,

Dispensing and Photographic Chemist,

57, HIGH STREET & **12**, KING STREET,

STROUD.   NAILSWORTH and CAINSCROSS.

"RODBOROUGH FORT,"
The striking landmark on the hilltop overlooking Stroud.

VIEW FROM WALL'S QUARRY, STROUD. *Photo by H. J. Comley.*

The Café Mid-Gloster,

20, GLOSTER STREET, STROUD.

WM. T. TUCK,

Pastry-Cook,
Confectioner,
. . Caterer,
Wine Merchant.

. Chocolatier,
Tea and Italian
Warehouseman,

Luncheon, Dining and Tea Rooms,

LADIES' AFTERNOON TEAS A SPECIALITY.

BRIDAL and **BIRTHDAY CAKES** have special attention.

WINES, ALES, STOUT, Etc., in Bottle and on Draught.

PLATE, etc., on Hire.

Hygienic Bakery - - - - - Bath Street.

Terms Moderate.   Estimates Free.   Your Patronage Solicited.

KING STREET PARADE, STROUD.

Photo by Smith.

THE SCHOOL OF ART, STROUD.

hot by Smith.

SIDNEY B. PARK,

MANTLES AND MILLINERY.

CORSETS AND UNDERCLOTHING.

MILLINERY SHOW ROOM.

GENERAL AND FURNISHING DRAPER,

BLACK AND COLOURED DRESSES.

CARPETS AND FLOORCLOTHS.

CARPET SHOW ROOM.

KING STREET and GEORGE STREET, STROUD.

GEORGE STREET, STROUD. *Photo by H. J. Comley.*

KING STREET, STROUD. *Photo by H. J. Comley.*

THE SUBSCRIPTION ROOMS, STROUD.   *Photo by Smith.*

KENDRICK STREET, STROUD.   *Photo by H. J. Comley.*

GEO. REDMAN & SON,

Tailors, Clothiers,
Outfitters,
Shirtmakers and Hosiers.

27, GEORGE STREET,
STROUD.

TAILORS. *We are PRACTICAL TAILORS. All work cut on the premises, and made by experienced workmen. Style and Fit guaranteed.*

CLOTHIERS. *A large and well-assorted stock of Men's and Boys' Suits, Trousers, Overcoats, etc. Private Showrooms for fitting on.*

OUTFITTERS. *GENTS' OUTFITTING of every description. Best Value at Popular Prices.*

SHIRTMAKERS. *SPÉCIALITÉ : OUR OWN MAKE SHIRTS. Made in Oxford, Regatta, Drill, Flannelette, etc.*

HOSIERS. *All the best makes of GENTS' HOSIERY kept in stock. PANTS and VESTS in every material and weight.*

—➤≡·∙≡◄—

GEO. REDMAN & SON, 27, George Street, Stroud.

INTERIOR OF THE PARISH CHURCH, STROUD. *Photo by Smith.*

LANSDOWN HALL, STROUD. *Photo by Smith.*

The Stroud Brewery

Established 1760.   Co., Limited,

THE BREWERY, STROUD.

And at Cheltenha r, Chepstow, Hereford, Newnham and Swindon.

Brewers, Wine and Spirit Merchants,
Pale Ale and Stout Bottlers, and
Aerated Water Manufacturers.

Celebrated Pure Bitter Ales
Mild Beers and Stout, Brewed from the finest materials, and having a high reputation for excellence. (Supplied in casks of all sizes).

Bottled Beers and Stout may be obtained in pints and half pints, in quantities of one dozen and upwards.

Wines and Spirits. —This Department is well stocked with a large and varied assortment of the choicest brands.

Aerated Waters of all descriptions.

Telegrams: "Stroud Brewery, Stroud."   Orders received by post or otherwise
Telephone 63.   have prompt and careful attention.

52

OLD ALMS HOUSES, CHURCH STREET, STROUD.   *Photo by H. J. Comley.*

THE OLD TOWN HALL, STROUD.   *Photo by H. J. Comley.*

House and Estate Agents, Auctioneers and Valuers.

DAVIS & CHAMPION,

16, KENDRICK STREET, STROUD.

Messrs. *Davis & Champion* make NO charge for inserting Properties for Sale or to Let in their *"Register,"* unless Purchasers or Tenants are found through that medium.

Fullest information given to those in search of Houses or Properties in the STROUD, Chalford, Bisley, Painswick, Gloucester, Cheltenham, Stonehouse, MINCHINHAMPTON, AMBERLEY, NAILSWORTH and DURSLEY districts.

BRANCH OFFICES :—   OFFICE HOURS: 9 a.m. to 6 p.m.
Dursley and Nailsworth.   Saturdays, 9 a.m. to 1 p.m.
LONDON ADDRESS :—10, Union Court, Old Broad Street, E.C.

The Hatter **T. F. TOMES** *23, King St.*
and Hosier **T. F. TOMES** *Stroud.*

Opposite
Royal George Hotel.
Established 1829.

SPECIAL HOUSE for...
**Light-weight Hats,
White and Coloured
Shirts,
Mackintoshes and
Rainproof Coats,
Gloves, Ties,
Collars, etc.**

SOLE AGENT for...
**The Celebrated
"Two Steeples"
Pure Unshrinkable
Wool Hosiery
and Underwear.**

SOLE AGENT for...
**"Dr. Jaeger's
Sanitary
Clothing"
Specialities
in Men's Wear.**

*Orders by Post promptly
attended to.*
Sample Shirt made in 24 hours.

54

Introduction.

To the Reader.

THE rapidity with which the first edition of "THE STROUD VALLEY ILLUSTRATED" was disposed of is a testimony to its popularity, and sufficient explanation of the necessity for a new and enlarged edition. That 10,000 copies should have been distributed in less than six months, is a circumstance highly gratifying to the Stroud Traders' Association, under whose

OLD HOUSE AT WHITMINSTER. *Photo by C. Upton.*

auspices it was produced, and the present opportunity may be taken for congratulating that useful association and the publisher on the success of their joint labours. In sending forth a second edition the promoters confidently appeal for renewed patronage, believing that by making better known the beautiful natural features of the Stroud district the prosperity of the inhabitants will be enhanced. Very flattering praise has been bestowed on "THE STROUD VALLEY ILLUSTRATED," and in its revised form it will, we are sure, afford even greater satisfaction.   THE EDITOR.

Visitors to Stroud should ask to see Burrow's "Royal" Series of Picture Postcards. Sold by Mr. W. Collins, 11, King Street, Mr. Elliott, Printer, High Street, Messrs. Lewis & Godfrey, Mr. John White, 23, George Street, Mr. James, Printer, Russell Street, also at Painswick and Amberley Post Offices.

Historic Stroud.

SIR ROBERT ATKYNS, the historian, described Gloucestershire as being divided into three districts—hill, vale and forest—entirely different from each other in the general character of scenery and inhabitants. The Stroud district partakes of all these features, for it lies in the heart of the county and is more or less influenced by the radius which surrounds it. In prehistoric times the Cotswold Hills and Valleys were doubtless densely wooded, giving rise to the word "Cotteswolds"—derived from the British "Coed" and the Saxon "weald," both signifying wood.

The fulling mills for which the Cotswold valleys have for generations been famous were directly due to the industry and energies of the Flemings, who, driven by persecution from their homes in the days of "Good Queen Bess," came here to settle and to enrich the natives by teaching them weaving and cloth-making. For example, the valley of the Froom was particularly busy in the sixteenth and two succeeding centuries. The discovery of steam-power and its application to machinery, however, induced the cloth-makers to forsake the lovely Cotswold districts for Midland and Northern centres in close proximity to the coal-fields. Thus the industrial character of Mid-Gloucestershire underwent a gradual change, and the monopoly of the district was virtually destroyed.

Stroud is one of the chief towns of what is known as the Vale, or Gloucestershire lowlands. An enormous amount of the land of the district was in the early ages in the hands of priories or monasteries—a priory at Leonard Stanley being amongst the richest of these monastic institutions. The monks encouraged their tenants in every direction, and, like all good landlords, watched their property greatly increase in value. There is every evidence that spiritual observances in this county were very regular, for the number of monasteries and churches gave rise to the saying, "As sure as God is in Gloucestershire."

William of Malmesbury, a reliable historian, was convinced that between eight and nine centuries ago Gloucestershire was rich in vineyards, and at Stonehouse there is a pasture south of the Parish Church still known as the "Wine Mead."

Unquestionably one of the chief inducements to the Flemings to settle in the Stroud valley was the quality of the water which flowed in the tributaries to the "Stroudwater," as it was called, and which gave permanency to the bright scarlet and blue dyes used in the manufacture of cloth. In the reign of Queen Mary, an Act of Parliament was passed which but for a special exemption in the case of Stroud would have borne heavily on the district. The object of the Act was to confine the manufacture of cloth to certain large towns, but when it was represented to the authorities that the weavers in the neighbourhood of Stroud were scattered over a considerable area, it was enacted that " it shall be lawful to all and every person or persons which now do, or hereinafter shall, inhabit or dwell in . . . . or in any of the towns or villages near adjoining the Water of Stroud, in the County of Gloucester, where clothes have been usually made by the space of twenty years past, and having been prentice to the occupation of cloth-making, or exercised in the same by the space of seven years, to set up, use and exercise the feat or mystery of making, weaving, or rowing of cloth, out of a city, borough, or market town as heretofore they might have done ; anything in this Act to the contrary notwithstanding." It may also be mentioned that the "rich clothiers of Stroudwater" are mentioned in connection with the Civil Wars in the seventeenth century. In the reigns of George III. and George IV. roads were made from Cheltenham to Painswick and from Gloucester to Stroud by way of Pitchcombe. The Great Western Railway from Cheltenham to Stroud and Swindon was constructed about the year 1840. The Midland line from Stonehouse to Nailsworth came much later.

Probably the oldest building in Stroud is the Town Hall, off High Street, now used for county court and petty sessions, and also for meeting of the Urban District Council. It is a very picturesque Elizabethan edifice and is a monument to the architectural tastes of the sixteenth century, at which period it was built by the lord of Lypiatt, John Throckmorton.

Stroud Parish Church, dedicated to St. Lawrence, stands close to the Town Hall. An ancient Chapel on this spot is mentioned in a deed of endowment dated 1304. This old chapel was added to from time to time, till it became the chancel of the Church. The church was rebuilt in 1867 at a cost of £8000. The steeple of the old building, which exhibited proofs of good fourteenth century work, was preserved and incorporated with the new ; the upper part of it has recently been rebult. The length of the church is 104 feet and the width of the nave and aisles is 66 feet, besides the projection of the transepts and the porch. It affords room for 1200 persons. It is of early English style, and is an unusually fine building.

Holy Trinity Church, Whitehall, was consecrated in 1839. It is 70 feet long by 45 feet wide and affords room for 700 persons. Its handsome school-room near by was erected and presented to the church by the Rev. G. T. Ormerod.

It has a Chapel of Ease at Thrupp, an iron building erected in 1889 at a cost of £1000.

All Saints' Church, Uplands, was erected by private generosity, and now belongs to the ecclesiastical parish of Slad.

THE HOSPITAL, STROUD.   *Photo by H. J. Comley.*

The Roman Catholic Church of the Immaculate Conception at Beeches Green, has a Convent (St. Rose of Lima), and school connected with it.

The Free Churches are well represented. The earliest Congregational Chapel is the Old Chapel, or "Old Meeting" as it was formerly called, in Chapel Street. It was built in 1710 and 1711, but worship had been carried on from 1687. A new front was erected to the chapel in 1844 at a cost of £800, and in 1881 it was further restored at a cost of over £1,800.

Bedford Street Chapel was built in 1835-36 at a cost of £3,000, and was opened in 1837.

The Wesleyan Chapel, in Castle Street, was opened October 27, 1876. It took the place of the old Wesleyan Chapel, in Acre Street, built in 1763, which was the scene of an annual visit of John Wesley till 1790. Wesley's first sermon in Stroud was preached standing on a butcher's block in the Shambles on Saturday, June 26th, 1742.

The old Wesleyan Chapel, which was called the Round Chapel, is now occupied by the Salvation Army.

John Street Baptist Chapel was built in 1824, and enlarged in 1879. A handsome new schoolroom has recently been erected by this congregation in Union Street at a cost of £1,350.

A second Baptist Church was formed in 1894, which occupies a building in Lansdown, formerly used as a Unitarian Chapel.

The Primitive Methodist Chapel, Parliament Street, was erected in 1836.

There are meetings of the Brethren in Acre Street, and Bath Street ; and a Hebrew Synagogue in Lansdown.

For further particulars and pictures of some of the best-known Nonconformist places of worship in Stroud, see page 97.

Bassevi designed the Subscription Rooms which were erected at the top of George Street in 1836, and were for many years the only place of public meeting. A curious story is told in connection with its erection. In order to facilitate the work a series of scaffolds, on the plan of a long inclined plane, were erected for the conveying of stones, mortar and other materials up the building. It commenced in Threadneedle Street near the yard of the Swan Inn. This inn was much frequented by farmers on market days ; and it happened that one Friday evening, farmer William Radcliff, of Woodchester, mounted his horse in the inn yard to return home ; but being somewhat under the influence of liquor, he (instead of turning in the right direction) rode to the bottom of the inclined plane, up which the horse walked, and carried his master to the top of the

BISLEY SPRINGS. *Photo by Smith.*

building. His perilous position was seen from below ; and, indeed, he himself became aware of it, and dismounted. It was thought by those who hastened to his assistance, that even the horse, if skilfully handled, might have been brought down unhurt, as well as his master ; but Radcliff persisted in backing the horse, which, under his management, fell from the scaffold and was killed. He himself came down in safety and withal a little sobered. In allusion to this event, the inclined scaffolding was jocularly called *Radcliff Highway.*

Badbrook Hall, intended for lectures and concerts, was opened in 1869. Lansdown Hall was erected in Lansdown in 1879, at a cost of £2,500, and more recently the Conservative party have provided at the top of Rowcroft, a club which has a large public saloon capable of holding 300 persons.

Within the past half of a century an enormous ready-made clothing trade has grown up in Stroud. The originators were the brothers George and Henry Holloway, originally master tailors of the town. They developed a business with branches all over the world. The principal factory is in Kendrick Street and Threadneedle Street, near the Subscription Rooms, and they have another large factory in Brick Row. A factory was carried on for some years off George Street by Messrs. Williamson, Tratt & Co., who in 1900 erected a large factory in Cheapside, to the South of the Great Western Station. The latter is now occupied by Messrs. Hill, Paul & Co., wholesale clothiers.

Lypiatt Park, on the road from Stroud to Bisley, a sixteenth century mansion, is the seat of Sir John Edward Dorington, Bart., M.P., chairman of the County Council. John Throckmorton owned it in the reign of James I., and there it is reported he and his confederates developed the Gunpowder Plot. The room supposed to have been used is still in evidence. The historic letter from Catesby to Lord Monteagle was said to have been written at Lypiatt.

The affairs of Stroud are administered by an Urban District Council. Two attempts have been made to procure a charter of incorporation for Stroud, but without success.

A monument to the late Mr. George Holloway, M.P., for the Stroud Division and founder of the Conservative Working Men's Association Benefit Society, stands at the top of Rowcroft. It was erected by public subscription, and was unveiled by Lady Dorington in 1895.

In Bisley Road stands the Cemetery, commenced in 1855 and enlarged in 1870.

A private club known as the Stroud Club, consisting chiefly of professional men, is held in the Subscription Rooms ; the Mid-Gloucester Conservative and Unionist Club is at the top of Rowcroft ; the Liberal Club is in Lansdown ; and a sporting club known as "The Stroud Borough Billiard Club," occupies premises in London Road.

The General Post Office, erected in 1885, is in Russell Street.

The Capital and Counties Bank stands at the bottom of High Street. There is a branch with resident manager at Nailsworth, and agencies at Chalford, Painswick, and Stonehouse.

Lloyds Bank is situated at Rowcroft, and has recently undergone extensive alterations.

The Wilts and Dorset Bank.

The Wilts and Dorset Banking Company, Limited, was established in 1835. The subscribed capital is £3,250,000, in £50 shares, the paid-up capital being

£650,000, and the reserve fund £750,000. The dividends paid during the last few years have been at the rate of 21 per cent. per annum. The head Office is at Salisbury, and there are now 143 branches and agencies, covering a wide district ranging from Portsmouth to Plymouth, and thence to Gloucester, and including branches at Stroud, Cheltenham, Cirencester, Gloucester, Nailsworth, Bristol, Cardiff, Clifton, Malmesbury, Swindon, and elsewhere in this neighbourhood. The Stroud office, a view of which is here given, is situate in George Street and is under the management of Mr. T. L. de Behr.

Stroud Incorporated Chamber of Commerce holds periodical meetings in the Subscription Rooms.

The Free Library, opened in 1888 in Lansdown, has a library of 3,000 volumes.

The School of Science and Art is in Lansdown, and contains one of the best equipped laboratories in the kingdom. An effort is being made to establish a public museum.

The principal newspapers of the district are the "Stroud Journal," which next year celebrates its jubilee, and the "Stroud News," established some years later than "The Journal," and "The Citizen" (Gloucester), and "Echo" (Cheltenham) are also circulated in the neighbourhood.

Stroud Hospital stands in a beautiful position at the top of Bowbridge lane, near Holy Trinity Church.

The Union Workhouse occupies a commanding site on the Bisley Road, from which may be obtained extensive views of the Severn Valley and the Welsh Mountains.

OLD ARCHWAY, STANDISH PRIORY, NEAR STROUD.   *Photo by C. Upton.*

There is a never-failing water supply by the Chalford Water Company. The town is at present illuminated by gas, and an electrical lighting scheme is under serious consideration.

Stonehouse, Chalford, Brimscombe, Tetbury, and Cirencester may be reached by the Great Western Railway ; and Nailsworth, Woodchester, Dudbridge, Ryeford, and Stonehouse by the Midland branch line. All other parts of the district can only be reached by conveyance. There is a regular service of 'buses to Stonehouse, Nailsworth, Painswick, Chalford and intermediate places, and a scheme is being promoted for the creation of an electric tramway linking Stroud to Chalford and Stonehouse, and possibly to Nailsworth and other places.

Stroud has two fire brigades—one supported by the Urban District Council, and the other consisting entirely of volunteer firemen.

The Society for the Prosecution of Felons is an old organization, remaining as a link with the pre-constabulary days.

In 1900 was formed the Stroud and District Traders' Association.

No other part of the country is richer in historic associations nor more pleasing to the eye in regard to varied and romantic scenery. The climate is so invigorating that hundreds of convalescents visit the district for final recovery, and Sanatoriums have been established at Cranham and Painswick for the open-air treatment of patients suffering from tuberculosis.

THE MIDLAND RAILWAY STATION, STROUD.

The Midland Station at Stroud was opened July 1st, 1886, by Mr. E. Allen, the present stationmaster. The branch railway from Stonehouse to Nailsworth was originally the work of a private company, and was taken over by the Midland Railway Company, which afterwards constructed the Stroud branch from Dudbridge. The Goods Department at Stroud was opened in November, 1885,

THE GREAT WESTERN STATION, STROUD.   *Photo by Smith.*

The Great-Western Station at Stroud was opened April 14th, 1845. The line from London was first constructed to Swindon, and was thence carried through to Gloucester and Cheltenham, at which time the station at Stroud was opened.

Stroud Post Office.

LETTER MAILS DESPATCHED.	Head Office Box Cleared.

F
- *Bristol and Stonehouse .... — 3-45 a.m.
- *Tetbury and Local Mails, including Town Delivery No. 1 .... — 5-45 ,,
- *London and places passing through......................... — 7-50 ,,
- *Gloucester and West of England .... — 8-45 ,,

A
- *London and places passing through................. .. ... — 9-10 ,,
- *Gloucester, Cheltenham and Town Delivery No. 2 .. .. — 9-50 ,,
- *Bristol, Bath, Warminster, etc., and Nailsworth.............. — 10-15 ,,

B *London, Swindon, Chippenham, Cirencester, etc. .... — 11-40 ,,

C *Cheltenham, Gloucester and Bristol .... — 12-50 p.m.

D
- *Local Day Mails .... — 1-30 ,,
- *Town Delivery No. 3 .... — 1-55 ,,
- *Stonehouse, etc. .... — 2-15 ,,
- *London, Cirencester, Oxford, Reading, etc. .... — 2-40 ,,
- *Cheltenham, Gloucester, Hereford, Worcester, Malvern, Birmingham, etc. .... — 2-40 ,,
- *Bristol, Bath and West of England .... — 4-45 ,,
- *Gloucester and Cheltenham .... — 5-15 ,,

E
- North Mail—London, East and S.W. England .... — 6-30 ,,
- *Town Delivery No. 4 (Week-days) .... — 7-15 ,,
- London and places passing through (Week-days)........ .... — 8-0 ,,

F
- Bath, Bristol, Chippenham, Hereford and West of England.... — 10-0 ,,
- South Wales, Gloucester and Cheltenham.................... — 11-30 ,,
- London Night Mail and East of England .... ⎱ 12-0 mid-
- Swindon, Cirencester, Reading, Oxford, etc................. ⎰ night.

STROUD POST OFFICE.   *Photo by H. J. Comley.*

Places marked *—Correspondence delivered same day.

Sunday Despatches—
See Mails E and F.

———

DELIVERIES IN STROUD.

1st Delivery—

London Night Mail and all parts .... 7-0 a.m.

2nd Delivery—

London, Gloucester and South of England .... 10-0 ,,

3rd Delivery—

From London, Cirencester, Gloucester, Cheltenham, Bristol, Stonehouse, etc. .. 2-0 p.m.

4th Delivery—

London and all parts .... 7-30 ,,

Sundays, 7 a.m.

Photo by *H. J. Comley.*

STROUD FROM RODBOROUGH.

Stroud : Its Situation.

THE Cotteswolds, which form the eastern side of the County of Gloucester, slope gently back into the levels of Oxfordshire and Wiltshire, and their western face overlooks the vale of Gloucester and the river Severn. This western face has numerous headlands and capes projecting into the vale, forming some beautiful bays, but it has no considerable inlet except near its upper end, where, at Sandford's Knoll, which is a bold projection connected with Frocester Hill, the vale of Stonehouse breaks into the range, and divides the northern from the southern Cotteswolds. This inlet is about two miles wide at its entrance and two miles deep, but contracts as it advances, and passing eastward into the mass of the Cotteswolds, is the approach to various tortuous gorge-like valleys, each of which, as it winds up into the range of hills, breaks into numerous smaller lateral valleys, and into combs, dells, and glens, having their own local names and peculiarities, and all being "beautiful exceedingly."

Stroud stands at the head of this inlet, and near it begin those gorge-like valleys, five in number, and known as the vales of Oozle's, Painswick, Slad and Steanbridge, Stroud and Chalford, and Nailsworth ; each of them having its stream of water with its tributary feeders, falling into the river Froom at Stroud. The spur of the Cotteswolds which separate these valleys from one another are Whiteshill, Wickeridge Hill, Stroud Hill, and the towering eminence of Rodborough Hill, crowned with the conspicuous building called The Fort, all stretching upward until they attain an equal height in the tableland of the range.

The great Vale of the Severn, with its wide expanse of gleaming water, backed by the Forest of Dean and the distant Welsh hills, presents from the heights of Frocester and Randwick such a magnificent picture as is probably unrivalled in England : whilst the inlet, or Stonehouse Valley, when viewed from the hills on either side, furnishes an interesting and beautiful scene of churches, mansions, manufactories, woods, meadows and water, with numerous villages, reposing on the sides and in the hollows of the hills, suggesting ideas of industry, wealth and social comfort.

The western boundary of the Cotteswolds, with its bold capes and headlands overlooking the Severn, may be compared to a long line of sea-cliffs ; and, according to Sir Roderick Murchison, it is probable that at a not very remote geological period the Severn Valley formed a gulf of the sea separating England and Wales, and that the entire region had been subsequently elevated, causing the retirement of the waters. The lateral Vale of Stonehouse must at that period have formed an inlet of the sea.

Stroud lies in the Hundred of Bisley, and became a distinct parish in 1360. Sir Robert Atkyns says: "It is so called from Strogd, which in the Saxon language signifies scattered, from their houses lying dispersed at a distance." At different periods the name has been spelt Strode, Strod, Strowed (where it occurs in the form of a well-known English word, of the same meaning as the original Saxon), Stroud.

It is the centre of the West of England clothing district, and in years gone by some of the finest cloth in the country was made there. It was said that the Stroud cloth would stand upright, and the only fault to be found with it was that it would not wear out. The Yorkshire cloth manufacture is now vastly more extensive, but a very large cloth business is still done in Stroud.

The population of Stroud itself is about 10,000. Within a radius of a mile from the centre there is an unbroken population of 20,000 ; and the valleys, from Stonehouse at the one extremity to Chalford and Nailsworth at the other, a distance of eight miles, have a population of over 40,000.

The river Froom (from the British word, ffrom, rapid), rises at Climperwell, and, after a circuitous route of about fourteen miles, reaches Stroud, where it receives its principal affluents, and falls into the Severn at Framilode, about eight miles below. In its course it gives name to Frampton Mansell, a hamlet of Sapperton ; Froom-mill and Froom-hall in Stroud ; Froombridge ; Frampton, which means the town on the Froom ; and Framilode, which means the exit or emptying of the Froom.

An Act of Parliament was obtained in 1727 for making it navigable from the river Severn at Framilode to Stroud, but the project was not carried out until 1775, when, under another Act, an independent canal was constructed. This canal has since been carried along the valley eastward, and by a tunnel through the hill at Sapperton, beneath the level of the railway tunnel, it is connected with the Thames at Lechlade.

C. A. DAVIS.

THE BLACK BOY SCHOOL, STROUD.   *Photo by H. J. Comley.*

Slad Valley, Birdlip, and Painswick.

THESE places may be appropriately linked together for the purpose of describing a walk which reveals some of the richest natural scenery to be found in the county of Gloucestershire. Less populous than the Nailsworth or Chalford valleys, that of Slad possesses distinctive points of beauty, which make it deservedly popular with lovers of the picturesque in Nature. There is no better example of a water-worn valley in the neighbourhood. Where now the little Slade meanders through a valley well stocked with alders and willows there must at one time have been a considerable volume of water. Denuding agencies have been at work for ages, with the result that much solid material has been washed away. Insignificant as the stream now is, it probably represents the most active force ·in the work of denudation. Although perhaps undeserving the name of a river, it has played an important part in the industrial history of this valley. Even now cloth mills standing on its banks find employment for a considerable number of hands, but this is at a point near the town of Stroud, and therefore before the most Swiss-like part of the valley is reached. Pedestrians should step aside to inspect New Mills Court, a substantial house built by Mr.

LANDSCAPE—SLAD VALLEY.   *Photo by Dr. Garrett.*

Thomas Bayliss in 1766. Once past the Woodlands, the eye travels over steep meadows, relieved by an occasional farmhouse. There is a fine belt of beech and larch wood on the crest of the ridge which divides Slad valley from Lypiatt. It comes to a termination at the bold barrier known as Swift's Hill. The oolitic rocks here offered a stronger resistance to the denuding agencies, which have given us Elcombe, close by, and Shepscombe, at a more remote point. It is a striking feature of the landscape, and from its summit may be obtained a fine view of Stroud and the Severn beyond. Here, too, in their season will be found the bee orchis, the fly orchis, and in late summer the small musk orchis. An exposure of the stratified rocks may tempt the geologist to use his hammer and chisel, and a section of the quarry is set forth in the late Mr. Witchell's " Geology at Stroud." Near the hill will be seen a few remains of what was once a large and important cloth mill. This gave employment to hundreds of people, many of whom came from Painswick, Shepscombe, Scrubbs, and the village of Slad. The latter is a very pretty spot, and might well tempt artists to reproduce its charms. Steanbridge House lies in an adjacent hollow, and is rendered desirable as a residence by a large piece of ornamental water. At the rear of the building will be found a road leading to the romantic hamlet of Scrubbs. Here, again, in pre-historic times the water hollowed out a glen which, with the hills on either side, suggests on a small scale scenes to be met with in mountainous districts. Passing up Bull's Cross Hill we shall see the steep lane along which Charles I. accompanied his cavaliers when bent on besieging the city of

OLD CLOTH HALL, MINCHINHAMPTON.　　　　　　　*Photo by C. Upton.*

Gloucester. From the Cross the monarch obtained a fine view of Painswick and its Beacon, beyond which lay the point towards which he was steering. If desirious of taking only a moderate walk, the pedestrian upon arriving at Bull's Cross will now turn to the left and return to Stroud by way of the old Painswick road. If, however, Birdlip and Cranham tempt him to travel farther north, he must brace himself for a more sustained effort. Once having gained the high tableland, he will find the view of surpassing beauty In the background is the town from which he started. Now we proceed in the direction of Birdlip, with Shepscombe and the Ebworth estate on our left. The latter should be seen in Autumn—

In that glad season, while his sweetest beams
The sun sheds equal o'er the meekened day.

It is then that we see

The fading, many-coloured woods,
Shade deepening over shade, the country round
Imbrown.

At Foston's Ash we are within easy reach of the Whiteway colony, but this would

PAINSWICK FROM THE CHURCH.   *Photo by H. J. Comley.*

EVENING AT PAINSWICK.   *Photo by Dr. Garrett.*

STROUD AND RODBOROUGH FROM FOLLY LANE.

take us off the Birdlip road. Cheltenham is six miles from Birdlip, and may be seen from different points. So, too, may the Malverns, the Wrekin in Shropshire, and Tewkesbury Abbey. The route from Birdlip to Cooper's Hill takes us past the Sanatorium, and on the same side in a hollow will be found Cranham, famous for its potteries. There is a tumulus in the woods within which were found skeletons of people who inhabited these parts long before the Romans saw the sun shining on the Severn valley and conceived the idea of building Gloucester. In this charming locality we are surrounded by evidences of the Roman occupation. Birdlip itself was probably a posting station. Here messengers would get a change of horses, and then pass rapidly over one or other of the straight roads which still remind us of the constructive power of the Romans. At Witcombe there is a Roman villa, but not equal to those of Chedworth or Woodchester. Having passed through Cranham Woods, we strike the Cheltenham road at the top of Cooper's Hill, and, turning to the left, make our way past Paradise, with Painswick Beacon on the right. This must have been a very important Roman camp, the well-preserved earthworks testifying to its great extent. If the hill be climbed, the traveller may look down on the spot where King Charles is reported to have said, in answer to the young Prince's inquiry, "When shall we go home?" "Alas, we have no home to go to." This was after the siege of Gloucester had been abandoned.

PAINSWICK CHURCH TOWER. *Photo by Smith.*

Painswick has a history of its own, as may be gathered from various sources. Situated almost on the crest of a hill, it justly enjoys a reputation for beauty. Its church and famous peal of bells, its stately yew trees, its Court-house and associations with Charles I., its quaint streets and quainter people, and, last but not least, its bracing air, which, if report speaks truly, is conducive to extreme longevity, all combine to make it a place well worth visiting. Here in 1535 King Henry VIII. was a visitor, and, according to an old letter, interested himself in a projected wood sale.

From Painswick to Stroud—the last portion of our walk—the scenery will still be found worthy of scrutiny. On the left we have Wickeridge Hill, and in the bottom of the valley the stream which supplies the pin mills of the neighbourhood with power. The whole district is well wooded, and may be regarded as scarcely less deficient in points of beauty to the adjoining valley of Slad.

WM. THOMPSON.

Drives or short Cycle Trips.

MINCHINHAMPTON FROM FORWOODS.

No. 1. Down Cainscross Road through Ebley towards Stonehouse, keep straight on under M. R. Bridge (4 miles) to Wheatenhurst Union; turn to left over Canal Bridge, up the hill through Eastington into Bristol Road (6 miles), turn to right towards Gloucester, keep on as far as the Cross Keys (11 miles) turn sharp to right into Stroud Road and return home through Standish and Stonehouse (20 miles).

This may be shortened by turning out of Bristol Road to the right at Whitminster, returning home *via* Nupend and Stonehouse (14 miles).

No. 2. Down Cainscross Road through Ebley, turn to left at Ryeford, through Kingstanley to Leonard Stanley (4 miles) on to Frocester (5 miles) proceed up Frocester Hill, turn to left at top of hill and home through Selsley and Dudbridge (13 miles).

This may be varied by turning to right at Frocester to Eastington and return home through Stonehouse, M R. end (11 miles).

No. 3. Down Cainscross Road, turn to left at Cainscross through Dudbridge into Nailsworth Road, on by Woodchester Station through Inchbrook to Nailsworth (4 miles), turn to left passing above Longfords to Avening (7 miles) on to Minchinhampton (9 miles) across the Common to Amberley and home down Butter Row (14 miles).

No. 4. Follow No. 3 to Dudbridge then up Selsley Hill, through Penn Woods to Nympsfield and into Bath Road, pass by Owlpen House, and return home through Horsley, Nailsworth, and Woodchester (17 miles).

No. 5. Along London Road through Brimscombe to Chalford (4 miles), up Cowcombe Hill to White Horse (6 miles) turn to right to Minchinhampton and return as No. 3 (12 miles) or through Amberley down Culver Hill into Nailsworth Road, and home through Dudbridge and Cainscross (13 miles).

No. 6. Along London Road to Brimscombe Station (3 miles) turn to left through Toadsmoor and Eastcombe to Bisley (6½ miles), return home down Bisley Road (11 miles) or continue from Bisley along Birdlip Road to Foston's Ash, and return home through Bull's Cross and Slad (13 miles).

No. 7. Up Slad Road, through Slad (3 miles) and Bull's Cross to Birdlip (9 miles) returning through Cranham Woods and Painswick (18 miles).

No. 8. Follow No. 1 as far as Bristol Road (6 miles), turn towards Gloucester, then to left through Frampton Green, Fretherne (9 miles) and Saul to Framilode-on-Severn (11 miles) returning through Whitminster, Nupend and Stonehouse (20 miles).

Outline List of the Flowering Plants found in the County of Gloucester.

N O apology is needed for describing this as a county list. It is true that many, and indeed some of the rarest, flowering plants of the county are found within walking distance, say eight miles of the town of Stroud. But to rigidly exclude all outside that radius would so limit the list that it certainly would not embrace all that might be found in a day's excursion.

There are many spots in the county within easy distance of Stroud, by rail or cycle, which contain some flowering plants peculiar to themselves, some of these spots from their position or from variety in the local geological formation are of great beauty also.

For example, Clifton Rocks and the Gorge of the Avon have a charm of their own, and form as well one of the richest parts of the county in floral varieties.

Then there is the far-famed Wye Valley, and its abundant flora ; the Forest of Dean ; the course of the Windrush, one of the feeders of the Thames in the north of the county, and in our more immediate neighbourhood Toadsmoor and the Chalford Valleys. The rare species they each contain could hardly be omitted from a complete list.

The orchid tribe may be quoted as an instance of the effect of any such omission. Twenty different species are to be found in the county, and of these sixteen are known to grow within four miles of the town of Stroud.

The list could hardly be considered complete if the four more distant species were not included.

The localities given in the list are not intended to show the exact habitat of each flower, but to indicate that it has been found near those places, and may be found there again.

In a few instances when the plant is extremely rare no locality is given.

The list is prepared from a larger one, but all the flowers mentioned have been noted growing in a wild state by the writer.

	Locality.
Pasque-flower Anemone, Anemone pulsatilla	Rodborough.
Meadow-rue, Thalictrum flavum	Brimscombe.
Bristol Rock-cress, Arabis stricta	Clifton.
Bitter Cress, Cardamine amara	Banks of streams.
Impatient-podded Ladies' Smock, Cardamine impatiens	Symonds Yat.
Narrow-leaved Wall Rocket, Diplotaxis tenuifolia	Sharpness
Lesser Wart-cress, Coronopus didyma	Woodchester.
Narrow-leaved Pepperwort, Lepidium ruderale	Amberley
Perfoliate Penny-cress, Thlaspi perfoliata	Sapperton.
Rock Hutchinsia, Hutchinsia petrea	Clifton
Woad, Isatis tinctoria	Very rare.
Marsh Violet, Viola palustris	Forest of Dean.
Water Chickweed, Stellaria aquatica	Woodchester.
Marsh Stitchwort, Stellaria palustris	May Hill.
Fine-leaved Sandwort, Arenaria tenuifolia	Stroud.
Marsh-mallow, Althœa officinalis	Bank of Severn.
Bloody Crane's bill, Geranium sanguineum	Forest of Dean.
Dusky Crane's bill, Geranium phœum	Near Painswick.
Mountain Crane's bill, Geranium pyrenaicum	Stroud.
Dyer's Green-weed, Genista tinctoria	Near Newnham.
Planchons Furze, Ulex Gallii	Forest of Dean.
Milk Vetch, Astragalus glycyphyllos	Henbury.
Least Bird's Foot, Medicago arabica	Forest of Dean.
Willow-leaved Spirea, Spiroea filipendula	Clifton.

	Locality.
Water Avens, Geum rivale	Brimscombe.
Spring Cinquefoil, Potentilla verna	St. Vincent's Rocks.
Great Burnet, Sanguisorba officinalis	Meadows by Severn.
Grass-leaved Vetch, Lathyrus Nissolia	Forest of Dean.
White Meadow Saxifrage, Saxifraga granulata	Chalford.
Alternate-leaved Golden Saxifrage, Chrysosplenium alternifolium	Painswick Valley.
Grass of Parnassus, Parnassia palustris	Bank of Windrush.
Navelwort, Cotyledon umbilicus	Cam.
Round and long-leaved Sundews, Drosera rotundifolia and intermedia	Mitcheldean.
Spiked water Milfoil, Myriophyllum spicatum	Brimscombe.
Wild Celery, Apium graveolens	Ditches near Severn.
Callous-fruited water Drop-wort, Œnanthe pimpinelloides	,,
Parsley water Drop-wort, Œnanthe lachenalii	,,
Fine-leaved water Drop-wort, Œnanthe phellandrium	,,
Dwarf Elder, Sambucus Ebulus	Woodchester.
Wild Madder, Rubra peregrina	Near Bristol.
Rough-marsh Bedstraw, Galium uliginosum	Woodchester.
Squinanchy-wort, Asperula cynanchica	Painswick.
Great wild Valerian, Valeriana Mikonii	Near Stroud.
Small Teazel, Dipsacus pilosus	Woodchester.
Mountain Everlasting, Antennaria dioica	Rudge Hill.
Elecampane, Inula Helenium	Cranham Wood.
Sea Wormwood, Artemisia maritima	Avonmouth.
Stinking Groundsel, Senecio viscosus	Sharpness.
Greater Burdock, Arctium majus	Stroud.
Woolly-headed Thistle, Cinicus ereophorus	Near Stroud.
Narrow-leaved Hawkweed, Hieracium umbellatum	Near Uley.
Ivy-leaved Bell-flower, Wahlenbergia hederacea	Forest of Dean.
Venus' Looking-glass, Specularia hybrida	Rodborough.
Creeping Bellflower, Campanula rapunculoides	Near Stroud.
Lesser Wintergreen, Pyrola minor	Randwick woods.
Yellow Bird's Nest, Hypopitys monotropa	Near Stroud.
Borage, Borago officinalis	Cheltenham.
Evergreen Alkanet, Anchusa sempervirens	,,
Corn Gromwell, Lithospermum arvense	Near Stroud.
Greater Dodder, Cuscuta europœa	,,
Deadly Nightshade, Atropa belladonna	Rodborough.
Henbane, Hyoscyamus niger	Forest of Dean.
Dark Mullein, Verbascum nigrum	Pitchcombe.
Sharp-leaved Fluellin, Linaria Elatine	Near Stroud.
Round-leaved Fluellin, Linaria spuria	,,
Spiked Speedwell, Veronica spicata	Clifton Rocks.
Ivy Broom-rape, Orobanche hederœ	Bank of Wye.
Lesser Broom-rape, Orobanche minor	Near Nailsworth.
Toothwort, Lathrœa squamaria	Near Bisley.
Bladderwort, Utricularia vulgaris	Near Tewkesbury.
Butterwort, Pinguicula vulgaris	Bank of Windrush.
Round-leaved Mint, Mentha rotundifolia	Wye Valley.
Peppermint, Mentha piperita	Near Stroud.
Larger Wild Thyme, Thymus chamœdrys	On most hills.
Calamint, Calaminta officinalis	Swift's Hill.
Clary or wild Sage, Salvia Verbenaca	Chalford.
Lesser Skullcap, Scutellaria minor	May Hill.
Horehound, Marrubium vulgare	Whiteshill.
Alpine Woundwort, Stachys alpina	Very rare.
Many-leaved Goosefoot, Chenopodium opulifolium	Near Stroud.
Fig-leaved Goosefoot, Chenopodium ficifolium	Near Cam.
Spurge Laurel, Daphne Laureola	In woods.
Bastard Toadflax, Thesium humifusum	Near Cheltenham.
Bushy-warted Spurge, Euphorbia stricta	Near Lydney.

FLOWERING PLANTS OF GLOUCESTERSHIRE.

	Locality.
Frog-bit, Hydrocharis morsus-ranœ	Ditches near Severn.
Bird's Nest Orchis, Neottia nidus-avis ..	Beech Woods.
Lady's Tresses, Spiranthes autumnalis ..	Swift's Hill.
Red Helleborine, Cephalanthera rubra ..	Very rare.
White Helleborine, Cephalanthera pallens ..	Near Stroud.
Purple Helleborine, Epipactis violacea ..	Very rare.
Green-winged Orchis, Orchis morio ..	Fretherne.
Bee Orchis, Ophrys apifera	Near Stroud.
Fly Orchis, Ophrys muscifera	,,
Musk Orchis, Herminium Monorchis ..	Selsley.
Butterfly Orchis, Habenaria chlorolenca ..	Near Stroud.
Angular Solomon's Seal, Polygonatum officinale ..	Chalford.
Streaked Field Garlic, Allium oleraceum ..	Bank of Avon.
Star of Bethlehem, Ornithogallum umbellatum ..	Dursley.
Snake's Head Fritillary, Fritillaria Meleagris ..	Fairford.
Meadow Saffron, Colchicum autumnale ..	Toadsmoor.
Sweet Sedge, Acorus Calamus	Stonehouse.
Flowering Rush, Butomus umbellatus ..	Near Chalford.

S. J. COLEY.

in Cranham Woods.

Edward J. Burrow 1896

JUDGE COX'S HOUSE, THE LYPIATTS, STROUD. *Photo by C. Upton.*

SHEEPSCOMBE, NEAR STROUD. *Photo by Dr. Garrett.*

Geology of Mid-Gloucestershire.

T HERE are few places where the Lower Jurassic rocks can be studied to greater advantage than the immediate neighbourhood of Stroud. Within a radius of ten miles from the town an almost complete series—from the Lower Lias beds, containing Ammonites Bucklandi, through the Middle and Upper Lias, the Cotteswold Sands, the Cephalopoda beds, the Inferior Oolite, the Fuller's Earth, the Stonesfield Slate, the Great Oolite, the Forest Marble, the Bradford Clay, and the Cornbrash—may be seen.

Within the limits available for this article it will be impossible to do more than to give a very brief summary of the various local formations, with their chief sub-divisions and more prominent characteristics, and to ind icate where the beds can best be studied. The reader will be presumed to have acquired a general knowledge of the strata referred to from the text-books and to have access to the Geological Survey maps of the district ; but a few references to books and papers treating more fully of the details of the Geology and Palæontology of the neighbourhood will be appended for the convenience of those who may be desirous of acquiring a more intimate knowledge of the subject.

Taking the formations in chronological order, then, we have the LOWER LIAS, comprising the following beds or zones :—

Zone of *Ammonites (Coroniceras) Bucklandi.*

This is the lowest zone which is exposed in the district. The best exposure is in the river cliff, known as Hock Crib, at Fretherne. The beds here consist of greyish blue limestone alternating with beds of extremely unctuous clay and shale. Large specimens of the characteristic Ammonite (*Cor. Bucklandi*) may occasionally be got, and *Arnioceras Bodleyi*, or a near ally, is by no means uncommon, but usually badly crushed and in the form of pyritized casts. *Gryphæa incurva* is very abundant and in fine condition. In the upper portion of the cliff is a bed containing great numbers of *Rhynconella triplicata—Quen.* This section can only be properly examined at low tide. Another small exposure of these beds occurs on the side of the road near Whitminster Church.

Zone of *Ammonites (asteroceras) Turneri.*
,,   ,,   (,,   ) *obtusum*
,,   ,,   (*oxynotoceras*) *oxynotum.*
,,   ,,   (*caloceras*) *raricostatum.*

Beds belonging to all these zones occur in the neighbourhood of Eastington, Standish and Stonehouse, but no sections exist. They can only be examinep occasionally when excavations are made for draining or similar purposes. They all consist of blue clay with occasional layers of limestone and shale.

MIDDLE LIAS.

Zone of *Ammonites (Uptonia) Jamesoni.*

There is no good exposure of these beds in the Stroud district. The road leading from Frocester to Coaley passes through a short cutting in a marly bed a short distance to the north of the first railway bridge. From the occurrence therein of *Waldheimia numismalis* and *Rhynconella rimosa* it is conjectured that the beds represent this zone. These fossils are, however, not conclusive.

Zone of *Amm. (Ægoceras) ibex.*

No exposure of these beds exists in the neighbourhood. Mr. Witchell, in his "Geology of Stroud," states that they were exposed at the Stroud Gasworks, and that a portion of a *I lesiosaurus* was found therein.

Zone of *Amm. (Liparoceras) Henleyi,* including the sub-zone of *Amm. (Liparoceras) capricornus.*

The beds constituting this zone consist for the most part of pale blue, some-

BURROW

Photo by H. J. Comley.

THE BRIMSCOMBE VALLEY.

what sandy clay with many ferruginous concretions. Large sections may be seen at the works of the Stonehouse Brick and Tile Company, adjoining Stonehouse Station (G.W.R.), and at the Standard Brickworks at Haywardsfield, also at the Lightpill Brickworks, near Dudbridge. They occur immediately beneath the marlstone of the Middle Lias (Margaritatus zone). Fossils are not common in the clay beds, but the irony nodules frequently contain Lamellibranchs and Belemnites. The characteristic ammonite *Lip. Henleyi* is seldom, if ever, found in the Stroud district. Occasionally large masses of impure limestone occur. Such a bed was opened up a few years since adjoining the Dudbridge Station on the Midland Railway, and produced a great number of beautifully-preserved fossils, including some good specimens of *Ægoceras latecosta*. Specimens of this ammonite are occasionally dredged from the bed of the canal in the neighbourhood of the gasworks

Zone of *Amm. (Amaltheus) Margaritatus.*

,,   *Amm. (Palt·pleuroceras) Spinatum.*

These two zones are treated of together, not on account of any difficulty in separating them, nor of any great similarity in their faunal contents, but because in this district wherever there is an exposure of the lower (Margaritatus) zone there is an almost certain exposure of the other. From the fossil collector's point of view, they are the most interesting (or, perhaps more correctly, the most prolific) of any of the Liassic series in this neighbourhood, and the sections are numerous. The two zones together constitute what is usually spoken of as the "marlstone" of the Middle Lias. Being composed of hard rock, the beds have resisted denudation to a greater extent than the clay upon which they rest, thus giving rise to an escarpment discernable almost everywhere around the foot of the hills as quite a distinct feature in the landscape.

The best sections in the immediate neighbourhood are those in the brickyards at Lightpill and in Rodborough Lane. In the former the rock is somewhat ferruginous, and contains many well-preserved Lamellibranchs and Belemnites, *B. paxillosus* and *B. apicurvatus* being particularly abundant in some blocks. In the Rodborough Lane pit the fossils are found in the hard concretionary nodules which are common in the clay, specimens of *Am. Margaritatus* being frequently enclosed in them, but very difficult to extract. Beautiful septarian nodules are not uncommon.

By far the finest sections of the marlstone, however, are those near the village of Stinchcombe, on the north-west side of Stinchcombe Hill. The marlstone has been quarried here for very many years, and all along the weathered faces of the workings beautifully-preserved specimens of *Rhyn. amalthei* project from the rock in thousands, together with numerous small specimens of *Pal. Spinatum* and other fossils. Fine large speci-

OLD CROSS AT BISLEY CHAPEL.   *Photo by C. Upton.*

mens of *Gryphæa cymbium* are not uncommon in the Lower (Margaritatus) beds, and several species of Waldheimia occur. In the Upper (spinatus) beds there is a regular layer of *Terebratula punctata*, but the specimens are usually crushed. Though fossils are numerically abundant, there is not the same variety as occurs in the Middle Lias of Somerset, and it is a singular circumstance that *Rhyn. tetrahedra*, which is usually so abundant in beds of this age in other localities, is extremely rare in the Stroud district.

UPPER LIAS.
Zone of *Amm.* (*Harpoceras*) *serpentinum.*
,, *Amm.* (*Hildoceras*) *bifrous.*

Although the Upper Lias has a considerable development in and around Stroud, it is very difficult to find a section for study. It lies everywhere upon the marlstone, but, being of small economic value, is not worked. The lower portion of the town is built upon it, and on rare occasions, when excavations for sewers or cellars are made, its fossils may be collected. A good section of the lower zone was opened a few years since when the "Stroud News" office was enlarged, and a considerable number of Ammonites (*Harpoceras falciferum*) were dug up, and the upper zone was well exposed in the excavation made for the erection of the new portion of Messrs. Godsell's brewery, from which some good examples of *Dactylioceras commune, D. Raquinianus* and *Hildoceras bifrous* were obtained. *Terebratula globulina* and *Rhynconella pygmæa* are said to have been found in the neighbourhood, but the writer has never been fortunate enough to find any. These small Brachiopods would be found in the lowermost beds immediately upon the marlstone. At Stroud the Upper Lias consists of stiff clay, but in Coaley Wood, near Uley Bury, it constitutes a portion of the "Cotteswold Sands." Towards the bottom of the picturesque lane leading from Uley Bury to Coaley is a bed of consolidated sand yielding *Hildoceras bifrous*, and a little higher up may be found *Dactylioceras crassum*. From the same locality the writer has obtained *Harpoceras bicarinatum*, but this is a very scarce fossil. A small section of Upper Lias clay may be seen resting on the marlstone near Stinchcombe. In former years, when the marlstone was being worked at this spot, many good fossils were obtained. Nailsworth Church stands upon the Upper Lias, and many specimens of the characteristic fossils were obtained when the church was erected. The outcrop of the Upper Lias may easily be traced around the hills by the springs which all break out at the junction of the Cotteswold sands with the clay beds.

Zone of *Ammonites* (*Lytoceras*) *Jurense.*
This zone comprises the greater portion of the Cotteswold sands and a series of limestone and shale beds of no great thickness overlying them, locally known as the "Cephalopoda beds." Mr. Buckman divides the zone into four sub-zones, which he distinguishes as—1. Variabilis beds (*Haugia variabilis*); 2. Striatulum beds (*Grammoceras striatulum*); 3. Dispansum beds (*Grammoceras dispansum*); and 4. Dumortieria beds (*Dumortieria* of various species). A few insignificant exposures of some of the beds occur on the north side of the Frome valley, but by far the best sections are to be found along the flanks of the hills to the south-west from the Pen Wood, Selsley Hill, to Uley Bury. They may also be examined on Cam Long Down and at North Nibley, and there is also a good section near Wotton-under-Edge. Perhaps the best section is that in the Long Wood, by the side of the old coach road. The beds are very prolific, but it is quite impossible in this place to give a list of the fossils which they produce. The preponderating forms are, of course, Ammonites, but there are also numerous Lamellibranchs and Belemnites, with some Gasteropods and Brachiopods, the latter including *Rhynconella cynocephala*, which is common in the upper beds.

Zone of *Amm.* (*Lioceras*) *opalinum.*
Two principal beds are included in this zone—the lower or "Moorei bed," containing as its dominant Ammonite *Dumortieria Moorei*, and the upper with numerous examples of *Lioceras opalinum*. Speaking generally, this zone may be studied wherever the Jurense zone is exposed. Both beds consist of limestones, the upper (opalinum) bed being usually very hard. Several other Ammonites occur besides some interesting Brachiopods—e.g., *Terebratula Haresfieldensis, Rhynconella cynocephala, Rhyn. Cotteswoldiæ,* and *Waldheimia Blakei.* The singular Belemnite *B. irregularis* is also a characteristic fossil of the Opalinum zone.

THE INFERIOR OOLITE.

It has been a fruitful source of discussion amongst geologists for many years past as to where the Inferior Oolite should be deemed to begin. By some the Jurense and Opalinum zones have been considered as Oolitic ; by others, as Liassic ; others again—and perhaps the wiser ones—say they belong to neither, and call them " Transition beds." Be it, however, as it may, we are on perfectly safe ground in stating that the strata above the Opalinum zone are Inferior Oolite. But another difficulty presents itself. The Inferior Oolite has been divided into a number of Palæontological zones, and the authorities are not quite in agreement as to how many of these zones there are. We will not attempt to settle the matter, but will adopt the older and, possibly, the more generally understood Lithological terms as far as it is possible to do so. As we are treating of only one district, this will not be difficult.

PEA GRIT SERIES.

Immediately on the top of the Opalinum beds comes a series of consolidated yellow sandstone beds of a few feet in thickness, which Mr. Witchell distinguished as "sandy ferruginous limestone." Fossils are not numerous, but, partly on that account and partly from their being—so far at least as regards the Brachiopods and Ammonites—transitional forms, they are of especial interest. The "zonal" Ammonite is *Tmetoceras scissum*, which, however, is extremely rare in the district. Far commoner are the Lamellibranchs *Modiola Sowerbyana*, *Greslya abducta* and *Pholadomya fidicu'a*, and a coral *Montliva'tia lens* is not rare. The beds are well exposed at Haresfield Beacon. Sections may also be seen at Long Wood, Frocester Hill, and Painswick Hill.

Next in order comes a thick series of limestones almost devoid of fossils, but with—at Painswick Hill—a nodular bed of about a foot in thickness containing clusters of *Rhynconella subdecorata*. The uppermost bed of limestone is more than usually fossilferous at Crickley Hill, and produces some good Brachipods, notably *Terebratula simplex* and *T. perovalis var.* These limestones may be seen at many places, Horns Valley, Selsley Hill, Randwick and Crickley being perhaps the best exposures.

Upon the limestone rests the "Pisolite" with its numerous fossils, comprising a great number of Echinoderms of many forms, of which *Pygaster semisculcatus* occasionally attains very large proportions. Brachiopods, with the characteristic *Rhynconella subangulata*, *R. oolitica*, *Terebratula perovalis*, *T. simplex*, and *T. plicata*, and a considerable variety of Lamellibranchs, several forms of Lima and Pholadomya being prominent. The Pisolite beds are most largely developed in the northern portion of the district, and die away entirely to the south-west of Selsley Hill. The finest section is at Crickley Hill, but they may be seen in Standish Park and at Painswick Hill and Randwick, and are represented at Selsley Hill by a reddish marly bed capping the limestones.

To the northward of Stroud the Pisolite is succeeded by a massive coral bed, well exposed at the Frith (Juniper Hill), Randwick, Edge Hill, near Shepscombe and at Crickley. From the red sandy marl which fills the hollows in many places many beautifully-preserved micro-organisms have been obtained comprising Brachiopoda, Bryoza, Ostracoda, and Foraminifera, including a number of as yet undescribed forms.

LOWER FREESTONE, OOLITE MARL AND UPPER FREESTONE.

This series is frequently grouped as the "Oolite Marl Series." The Lower Freestone produces the principal building stone of the district and is extensively quarried. From the collector's point of view, however, it is not interesting, as it is almost devoid of organic remains. The Oolite marl, on the contrary, is absolutely useless economically, but very prolific in the matter of fossils. The Upper Freestone is not always present, and is really only a portion of the Oolite marl consolidated. The faunal sequence of the Oolite marl has been very carefully worked out, and each bed may be distinguished by its own particular Brachiopods. Among the most important of the Brachiopoda may be mentioned *Terebratula fimbria*, *T. submaxillata*, *T. curvifrons*, *Rhynconella subobsoleta*, *R. Tatei*, *R. cyn morpha* and *Waldheimia Leckenbyi*. The Lower Freestone may be seen in most of the hillside quarries around Stroud. The best section of the Oolite marl will be found at the Firth (Juniper Hill), but good sections are open at Stroud Hill (Conegre Quarry), Swift's Hill, Rodborough Hill and Selsley Hill.

BURROW

THE VIEW FROM SELSLEY HILL.

LOWER TRIGONIA GRIT.

This bed has not until recently been recognised near Stroud. It, however, undoubtedly exists, and may be seen at Swift's Hill and Juniper Hill, whence some good tabulate corals have been obtained. It is well exposed at Crickley. The Lower Trigonia Grit is chiefly notable for the number of Lamellibranchs which it contains. A few Ammonites of the " Discitæ " group have also been found, but they are rare in the Cotteswolds. Brachiopods, too, are far from common ; a very characteristic one, however, *Waldheimia meriani*, occurs at Crickley, but has not been found nearer Stroud.

THE BUCKMANI GRIT.

This, although an important and productive formation at Leckhampton, is but feebly developed in the Stroud area. It may be distinguished at the Frith and Swift's Hill as a thin layer of yellow incoherent sand. On Painswick Hill it is considerably thicker, and in Cranham Wood, near Buckholt Lodge, is a good section. A very prolific exposure was until lately exhibited near the " Air Balloon " at Crickley, but this is not now worked. The bed contains several peculiar Brachiopods, notably *Terebratula Buckmani*, *T. Crickleyensis*, *T. Uptoni*, and a small spinose, *Rhyncho ella (Acanthothyris sp.)*. which is the earliest spinose form known in the Cotteswolds.

THE GRYPHITE GRIT.

The Gryphite Grit is the lowermost of the beds usually known as the " Ragstones." It contains few fossils other than the well-known *Gryphæa sublobata*, which, however, is very abundant. This shell is also found in the Upper Trigonia Grit, and for this reason it is not always easy to indicate the dividing line between the two beds. The Gryphite Grit is exposed in most of the quarries on the upper parts of Stroud and Rodborough Hills. Many of the " Toppers," or rough capping stones, which are placed on dry Ragstone walls, are from this bed.

THE UPPER TRIGONIA GRIT.

Perhaps the most fossiliferous of all the Inferior Oolite rocks of the Cotteswolds. It is quarried for road stone and dry-walling on all the hills in the district. Fossils are extremely abundant both numerically and specifically. Of the Brachiopods *Terebratula globata*, with its numerous varieties, may be collected in thousands. *Acanthothyris spinosa* is also very common. Others are *Rhynconella Hampenensis*, *R. angulata*, *R. subtetrahedia*, *Aulocothyris carinata*, *Zeiller a Hughesi*, and *Z. Waltoni*. Lamellibranchs of many kinds abound, and a few Echinoderms are found. Ammonites of the Parkinsoni Group are occasionally met with.

THE CLYPEUS GRIT.

Resting on the Upper Trigonia Grit in many of the quarries is a series of rubbly beds known as " Clypeus Grit," so called from the occurrence therein of the large Echinoderm *Clypeus Plottii*. This fossil is more abundant in the North Cotteswolds than in the Stroud district, but it is occasionally found. The Brachiopods, on the whole, resemble those of the Upper Trigonia Grit, the most marked difference perhaps being the absence of *Acanthothyris spinosa*. A few Echinoderms occur, including the rare *Magnotia Forbesi* and *Polycyphus Normannus*. The lower bed of the Clypeus Grit is locally a coral bed.

THE GREAT OR BATH OOLITE SERIES.

We have now left the Inferior Oolite, and will proceed to describe briefly the next and, for Stroud, last of the Jurassic Series.

THE FULLER'S EARTH.

Except where denudation has extended down to the Inferior Oolite, the Fuller's Earth exists everywhere, separating it from the Great Oolite limestones. Sections are, however, scarce, as it has no economic value. It is, nevertheless, a very important bed on account of the water supply which it furnishes, and its outcrop may easily be traced by this means. Were it not for the Fuller's Earth, Amberley and numerous other places on the hills would have no existence. Palæontologically in this district it is not very interesting, almost the only fossil being *Ostrea acum.nata*, which may, however, be obtained in abundance in masses from the sections by the sides of some of the lanes in the neighbourhood of Amberley.

GEOLOGY OF MID-GLOUCESTERSHIRE.

THE STONESFIELD SLATE.

The principal exposures of these beds are Trougham Field, near Miserden, where the "Tiles" have been quarried for centuries. Many of the old houses in the neighbourhood are covered with "stone tiles" from these beds. On many of the slabs crushed Lamellibranchs may be found, and very rarely specimens of *Astropecten Cottswoldiæ*.

THE GREAT OOLITE LIMESTONES.

Economically this is one of the most important of the local formations, as it furnishes the best building stone of the district. It is extensively quarried on Minchinhampton Common and on the opposite hill at Quarhouse and Bussage, and fine sections may be seen at each of those places. The late Dr. Lycett made a large collection of fossils from the quarries on Minchinhampton Common, and by carefully looking over the waste from the workings the collector may in a few hours obtain hundreds of specimens of small Lamellibranchs and Gasteropods. Brachiopods are very scarce, but occasional valves of *Terebratula intermedia* may be found, and *Rhynconella concinna* also occurs. Ammonites and Belemnites are very rare indeed, but fairly good corals are not uncommon in one of the beds, and Echinoderms are occasionally met with.

REMAINS OF PIT DWELLINGS ON SELSLEY HILL, STROUD.   *Photo by C. Upton.*

THE FOREST MARBLE.

A series of flaggy beds resting on the more massive beds of the Great Oolite may be seen to the east of Minchinhampton in roadside quarries, from which road material is quarried. The fossils are not very interesting to the collector, consisting very largely of small crushed oysters. Sections may be seen near the Park, Minchinhampton, and about a mile further east than the "Ragged Cot." In a field near Gatcombe Park, adjoining the road from Minchinhampton to Avening, is a good section where may be seen a bed of clay crowded with large specimens of *Rhynconella obsoleta* and small oysters. This clay bed may represent the Bradford clay, but as it does not produce the characteristic Brachiopods of that formation, it is somewhat doubtful.

THE BRADFORD CLAY.

The only exposure in this neighbourhood other than the doubtful one before referred to is by the roadside, adjoining the Great Western Railway at Tetbury Road Station. From this section have been obtained *Rhynconella obsoleta, Eudesia cardium. Waldheimia digona* and *Dictyothyris coarctata,* and a number of small oysters and other Lamellibranchs.

THE CORNBRASH.

A small section of this formation occurs in the railway cutting east of Kemble Junction, but it is not exposed at any other place within the radius selected. South and east of Cirencester there are numerous exposures. The Cornbrash is the most recent of the Jurassic formations occurring in the district of Stroud.

This article would be incomplete without some reference to the gravels; but the subject is so extensive that it will be impossible to do more than state that there are extensive beds of rolled river gravel along the northern side of the valley of the Frome at Bowbridge, and from Stroud westward as far as Stone-house with occasional breaks. At Stanley Downton is an elevated tract of land containing a bed of similar gravel. Another extensive bed occurs near Standish, and still another near Frampton-on-Severn. The gravel consists of rounded fragments of the Great and Inferior Oolites, but in the Frampton beds there is a considerable admixture of Lower Lias limestone, and specimens of *Gryphæa incurva* may be found in it. From the neighbourhood of Stroud a considerable number of teeth and tusks of mammoth have been obtained. Good sections may be seen near Gannicox, Cainscross and Stanley Downton, and also by the road-side leading from Eastington to Frampton-on-Severn. There is also a good section at Nailsworth.

The following are some of the books and papers bearing on the geology of the district which may be consulted with advantage :—

Lycett.—The Cotteswold Hills. This work was published in 1857 and is somewhat out of date.

Witchell, E.—The Geology of Stroud. 1882.

Woodward, H. B.—The Geology of England and Wales. 1887.

Morris and Lycett.—The Great Oolite Mollusca and Supplement. Palæontographical Society. 1851—1863.

Davidson, T.—The Fossil Brachiopoda. Pal. Soc. Vols. I., IV., and V.

Lycett, Dr.—The Fossil Trigoniæ. Pal. Soc.

Wright, Dr.—The Liassic Ammonites. Pal. Soc.

Buckman, S. S.—The Inferior Oolite Ammonites. Pal. Soc.

Huddleston, W. H.—The Jurassic Gasteropoda. Pal. Soc.

Buckman, S. S.—The Cotteswold, Midford and Yeovil Sands. Q.J.G.S. Vol. XLV. (1889), p. 440.

Buckman, S. S.—The Bajocian of the Mid-Cotteswolds. Q.J.G.S. Vol. LI. (1895), p. 388.

Numerous papers by Lucy, Witchell, Buckman and others in the procedings of the Cotteswold Naturalists' Field Club.

CHARLES UPTON.

Archæological Notes on the District.

By CHAS. UPTON.

O the Archæclogist the Stroud district affords a good field—whether his taste lies in the direction of prehistoric remains or of relics of historic times, the visitor will have no difficulty in finding abundant material.

The remains of Antiquity group themselves naturally into two sections, viz., those belonging to prehistoric—which for England is equivalent to pre-Roman—times, and those dating from the time of the Roman Invasion.

It is true that Stroud cannot boast of any objects of such magnificence as Stonehenge or the Avebury Circle, nor is there anything equal to the Menhirs and Dolmens of Carnac or the superb chambered tumulus of Maestrowe in Orkney, but of pit-dwellings, tumuli—both round and long—camps and earthworks there is a good store.

PIT DWELLINGS. These occur in hundreds on the tops of Rodborough and Selsley Hills and on Minchin-hampton Common. At the present day all that can be seen is a number of depressions in the surface of the Common, varying from one to two feet in depth, twelve to twenty feet in length and four to ten feet in width, each of which has a mound on one side of approximately the same dimensions. Several of these structures have been explored from time to time, and from the fact that charcoal is usually found in them, and not unfrequently indications of a fire-place, it may be safely assumed that they were habitations of the living and not receptacles for the dead. As to whether the pits were covered by any sort of roof nothing is known, but as wood was abundant it is not unreasonable to assume that branches of trees—possibly with skins stretched over them—may have been used so as to obtain greater protection than was afforded by the mere mound of earth. The accompanying photo (page 49) will give an idea of the present-day aspect of these structures.

Round Tumuli. These were formerly very numerous, scattered generally about the higher portions of the district, but unfortunately the majority have now disappeared, having been ploughed down. A number of those which remain have been opened for the purpose of investigation and have consequently lost their interest. There are, however, still a few remaining undisturbed, two of the most conspicuous being situated near to each other on the summit of a small hill immediately to the westward of Standish Railway Bridge. In general appearance these tumuli consist of circular mounds of from fifty to sixty feet in diameter and from three to five feet in height. The Round Tumuli are not chambered, but appear to be mere mounds of soil or rubble heaped up over the charred remains of the individual, whose place of sepulchre they indicate. The builders of these mounds appear to have practised cremation, as in most, if not in all, which have been opened charcoal and burnt bones have been found, and occasionally flint chips and arrowheads of palæolithic type. The charred fragments of bone are invariably found at the centre of the mound, occasionally in a small hole scooped out in the original surface of the ground, but more frequently lying directly upon the surface.

Long (or Oval) Tumuli. A considerable number of these exist. All have been opened, but the mounds retain pretty much their original size and shape. In the majority of cases nothing can be seen of the interior but in some which will be mentioned presently the chambers still exist and may be inspected. Among the more accessible of these barrows may be mentioned the following :— Uley Bury Tumulus, sometimes known as " Hetty Pegler's Tump," near Uley Bury, " The Toots " on Selsley Hill, " Whitfield's Tump " on Minchinhampton Common, Bown Hill tumulus, Gatcombe tumulus, one in Cranham Wood, and one in Randwick Wood above the village of Ruscombe. In a field at Nymphsfield, opposite to the entrance to Woodchester Park may be seen the stones which formed the chambers of a barrow of this type which were uncovered in 1862, and left standing in their original positions. In this tumulus were found bones indicating the interment of at least thirty-two bodies, together with a few fragments of pottery and flint flakes. In the year 1806, a large oval tumulus which stood in a field near the Avening Rectory was uncovered, and the three chambers which it contained were removed and re-erected in the relative positions in which they were found in a grove near the entrance to the Rectory grounds where they still remain. One of these chambers is peculiar in having a circular aperture at one end.

Of the long barrows mentioned above, perhaps the best known and most interesting is the Uley Bury tumulus. It is situated on the apex of a promontory about a quarter of a mile to the north of Uley Bury and is a very conspicuous object. Most of the chambers remain intact and may be entered. A considerable number of human bones were found in this tumulus. The mound is enclosed by iron fencing, but the key of the gate is kept at the cottage adjoining Uley Bury and may be obtained on payment of a small fee, and may I here beg the visitor to treat the monument with the reverence to which its age entitles it. Gatcombe tumulus is another mound, the chamber in which remains intact. This tumulus is situate about half a mile south from the town of Minchinhampton.

A ROMAN ALTAR FOUND NEAR NAILSWORTH (now in the possession of Mr. A. E. Smith). *Photo by C. Upton.*

ARCHÆOLOGICAL NOTES ON THE DISTRICT.

The long barrows are considered to be of later date than the round barrows and the bodies of those buried in them do not appear to have been cremated.

CAMPS AND EARTHWORKS. On almost every one of the spurs of the Hills which overlook the Severn Valley an extensive and important camp is situated. Probably all or most of them were occupied and used by the Romans for the purpose of keeping in check the inhabitants of the country across the Severn, but there is little doubt that the Camps existed prior to the Roman occupation and that the Romans merely occupied them adapting them to their needs.

Within the Stroud district there are fortified Camps at Wotton-under-Edge, Stinchcombe Hill, Uley Bury (a remarkably fine example), Haresfield, Painswick (Kinsbury Castle), Cooper's Hill, and Crickley Hill. All of them are in a good state of preservation.

Uley Bury is the most important of these Camps. It occupies the entire area of a small hill projecting from the main mass immediately to the north of the village of Uley. The Camp is surrounded by two banks and ditches which follow along the crest of the hill, the area within the fortifications being upwards of thirty acres in extent. The shape is approximately a parallelogram, and at the northern angle the camp is connected with the adjoining hill by a narrow isthmus of about fifty yards in breadth protected by a triple arrangement of trenches and banks extending across it. Two other entrances protected by

THE "LONG STONE." *Photo by C. Upton.*

earthworks existed at the eastern and southern angles of the camp. In pre-artillery days this camp must have been practically impregnable, and from the extent of country overlooked by it, a place of very considerable importance.

Painswick Camp, or as it is usually called Kimsbury Castle, is another prominent and well-preserved camp. On the north side it is protected by a natural steep declivity, but on all other sides there are double lines of defence. Within the area of the camp the Well for supplying it with water can be seen.

Haresfield Camp occupies a very commanding position about midway between Uley Bury and Kimsbury Castle. This camp is interesting from the circumstance that it bears evidence of having in its original condition been more extensive than was deemed necessary by its later occupants the Romans. As originally constructed it comprised the peninsular-like prominence, now known as " The Beacon " together with a considerable area of the main mass of the Hill behind. The older line of entrenchment still exists across the fields some two or three hundred yards eastward from the isthmus, while the later and much loftier line merely extends across the isthmus. On the other sides the steep slope of the hill was mainly relied on for defence. A protected way leads into the camp on the south side.

The principal earthworks other than the well-defined camps already mentioned are situated on Minchinhampton Common. Immediately above Amberley on the top of the hill there is a mound and ditch which running south-east, south, and south-west, encloses a (roughly) semi-circular portion of the common of about fifty acres in extent. Across this enclosure rather to the northward of the centre is another mound dividing the enclosure into two parts. About half a mile eastward is another more important line of entrenchments which commences above the village of Box, and runs thence in an almost northerly direction nearly across the Common, turning abruptly to the east near the road from Rodborough to Cirencester. At the angle is an opening which appears to be part of the original design. This earthwork is believed to be of later date than the one near Amberley, indeed, a recent writer has ascribed it to the Danes. On Selsley Hill, a low mound and ditch commences close to the Pen Wood, whence it runs northerly for a considerable distance and then turns easterly at a right angle extending practically across the hill. It is worthy of note that of the great number of pit-dwellings on Selsley Hill not a single one is found to the southward of the entrenchment, whilst on Minchinhampton few, if any, are to be found within the (so-called) Danish Camp. Smaller earthworks exist at other places, e.g., Randwick Wood near the long barrow mentioned above and in Standish Park.

In a field near to the Gatcombe tumulus there stands a large monolith known as the "Long Stone." The portion which projects above the ground is about seven feet in height. This stone is popularly believed to mark the spot where a Danish chief was killed, but this in the writer's opinion is very doubtful. There were formerly two other similar stones near ; one of them has entirely disappeared and the other—a much smaller one—is incorporated in the wall dividing the field from the road.

The hollow immediately to the southward of the "Long Stone" is known as "Woful Danes Bottom" and there is reason to believe that at this spot was fought a great battle between the Saxons and the Danes in the year A.D. 837.

Of Roman remains few examples are to be seen in the immediate vicinity. One of the finest villas known in the country exists at Woodchester. It lies partly under the churchyard and partly under adjoining property —unfortunately it is entirely covered up. It is matter for regret that this magnificent example cannot be uncovered and protected somewhat in the manner in which the villas at Chedworth at Witcombe have been. The last time this villa was displayed was in 1890, when a considerable portion in the churchyard was uncovered. A pamphlet with a plan of the whole villa and coloured drawings of some of the details of the tessellated pavements was published at the time by the Rector of Woodchester, of which copies may possibly still be procured of Mr. John White, George Street.

A small but very interesting Roman villa exists at Witcombe not far from Buckholt Cottage. This has been

FROCESTER TITHE-BARN.　　　　　　　*Photo by C. Upton.*

carefully protected by the erection of a thatched building over it and may be inspected.

Chedworth Villa though not exactly within the Stroud district can be visited within a day, and is so unique that no visitor should leave the neighbourhood without seeing it. The remains which include some very perfect tessellated pavements and bath, almost as complete as when in use, perhaps sixteen or seventeen centuries ago, are very extensive, and there is also a museum attached in which may be inspected a large collection of objects which were found during the process of excavation. The villa may be reached from Foss Bridge Station, from which it is distant about two miles, or from Cirencester by a charming drive of about seven miles.

Of later objects of interest space will not permit me to do more than indicate a few.

Churches naturally come first. Of these the most interesting on account of their age are Avening, Leonard Stanley and Elkstone, near Birdlip. Painswick, Minchinhampton, Bisley, and Sapperton are also replete with interest. In Minchinhampton Church are some interesting brasses, and here was buried Dr. James Bradley, the Astronomer Royal. In Sapperton Church is a fine monument to Sir Robert Atkyns, the Gloucestershire Historian and Topographer.

Of Berkeley Castle, which is sometimes open to visitors, I need say nothing. Beverstone Castle which in the troublous Reign of King Charles I., was garrisoned for the King and besieged by Colonel Massey is also an interesting ruin.

The Spacious Tithe Barns at Frocester and Calcot near Nailsworth are reminders of the times when Tithes were paid in kind, and, if one may judge from their capacity, of times when the clergy were well-to-do, and may well claim the visitor's attention as may also what remains of the Conventual Buildings at Leonard Stanley and Standish.

Of the domestic Architecture of the fifteenth, sixteenth, and seventeenth centuries it is impossible to speak in detail. It is to be found everywhere throughout the district.

REMAINS OF THE ROMAN VILLA AT CHEDWORTH.   *Photo by Dr. Garrett.*

Church Bells of Mid-Gloucestershire.

'Tis but a village bell! yet oh! how strange
Its import, 'midst the varying scene around,
The cot, the cabin, mansion, hall and grange,
Obey the solemn magic of its sound,
In life and death alike, till all in Heaven are crowned.
"VANGUARD" (*T. Winter Wood*).

HE neighbourhood of Stroud abounds in churches, many of which contain peals of four, six, eight, ten, and in one instance twelve bells. Many of these are pre-Reformation, and therefore dedicated to some saint. Others bear inscriptions, and are dated, and on them are inscribed the names of the churchwardens in office at the time they were fixed, as well as those of the bell-founders who cast them. A great many of the Eighteenth Century bells were cast by the county firm—the Rudhalls, of St. Michael's Parish, Gloucester.

ST. LAWRENCE, STROUD.

The Parish Church of Stroud contained in 1629 six bells. Five of these were re-cast in that year by a bell-founder named Roger Purdue, who received £12 in payment, and this charge included "digging and carriage of earth for to cast the bells," as well as "cole and wood" to melt them. The bells were tuned at this time by a Mr. Kirby, who received ten shillings therefor. The 6th bell was re-cast in 1713.

On a fly-leaf of the old Churchwardens' Book the weight of these old bells is thus given :—

	cwt.	qrs.	lbs.
The tenor, being ye 6th bell, wayeth	14	1	24
The 5th bell wayeth	14	1	24
The 4th bell wayeth	11	0	18
The 3rd bell wayeth	09	0	9
The 2nd bell wayeth, which was not cast nor wayed	08	3	2
The 1st, or treble bell, wayeth	08	3	2

Some time previous to 1814 two more bells seem to have been added. In that year the tenor bell fell whilst being rung in peal, and was fractured, also splitting the eighth bell, consequently the two required to be re-cast. At the same time, the inhabitants subscribed for the casting of two more bells, thus completing the present peal of ten. The old tenor which fell bore the following inscription :—

"Come when I call; God bless you all."

The following are the inscriptions on the present bells :—

The Tenor.—"May all whom I summon to the grave,
The blessings of a well-spent life receive."
W. C. CHAMBERS, Esq., and RICHARD COOK, Churchwardens, 1815.
THOMAS MEARS, London, Fecit.

No. 1, The Treble.—"In sweetest sound let each its note reveal,
Mine shall be first to lead the dulcet peal."
W. C. CHAMBERS, Esq., etc.

No. 2.—"We come with harmony to cheer the land,
The public raised us with a liberal hand."
W. C. CHAMBERS, Esq., etc.

No. 3.—"Prosperity to all my benefactors."

No. 4.—"Prosperity to all my friends."

No. 5.—"Prosperity to this parish."

No. 6.—"Prosperity to this place."

No. 7.—"WILLIAM KNIGHT, Esq., and Mr. RICHARD ALDRIDGE, Churchwardens, 1771."

No. 8.—"May all whom I summon to the grave,
The blessings of a well-spent life receive "

No. 9.—"JOHN LONG and HENRY COOK, Churchwardens, 1721.
Cast by ABRAHAM RUDHALL, of Gloucester.

Stroud people are nothing if not loyal. At the Restoration of the Monarchy under Charles the bells were rung, and the ringers received 2 shillings ! They were also rung at the capture of the Duke of Monmouth, when the ringers received 10 shillings, and again at the conclusion of the trial of the seven bishops, when they again received 10s.

MINCHINHAMPTON (4 miles S.S.W. from Stroud).

The Church of Holy Trinity possesses in its truncated spire six bells, of which some have been recast. The following are the weights of the bells, with the legends on them :—

No. 1.—The Treble is in the key of D sharp and weighs 5½ cwt. Its legend is " Peace and good Neighbourhood ". A · R 1719.

No. 2.—Is in the key C sharp and weighs 6 cwt. The inscript on is "GEORGE PLAYNE and FRANS. CHAMBERS, Churchwardens, 1842. T. MEARS, Fect."

No. 3.—Is in the key of B, and weighs 7 cwt. Its legend is " Prosperity to the Church of England." NATH. PERKS and JAMES PARKER, Churchwardens. A R 1736.

No. 4.—Is in the key of A sharp and weighs 8 cwt. Its inscription is " A. TOWNSEND and G. RALPH, Wardens, 1797. J. RUDHALL, Fect."

No. 5.—Is in the key of G sharp and weighs 9½ cwt. Inscription, "JOHN ROMDEN, Curate, A R 1719."

Tenor is in the key of F sharp and weighs 13 cwt. Its inscription is " JOS. ILES and JACOB SCUSE, Churchwardens, 1825."

LEONARD STANLEY (4 miles S.W. from Stroud).

This Church is dedicated to St. Swithin, and was anciently connected with a Benedictine Priory, founded here by one of the lords of Berkeley in 1146. In its diminutive tower are four bells hung in a fine ornamental frame, two of which are pre-Reformation. In the year 1538 they became the property of the parishioners of Leonard Stanley by purchase. There is a deed still extant by which the Abbot of Gloucester conveyed them on payment of " xxx pounds of lawful money of England " to " the hole parishoners of Leonard Stanley." The bells bear the following legends :—

1st Treble + Missi : De : Celis : Haboo : Nomen : Gabrielis.
2nd Ora : Pro : Nobis : Lanche + Law (Ib.N.F. ?)
No. 3.—Lord by Thy might   keep us   from Poope   and Hypocrite   1678.
No. 4.—Tenor   R. P.   W. C.   GEORGE   WRIGHT, JOHN BARRONS, Church Wardens.   1678.   On the upper line is : In   Honorem   St. Petri Fecit   Fieri.

The initials on the tenor bell stand for R. PACKE and W. CHAPMAN, well-known bell-founders in the 17th century. The last legend was probably copied from an older bell, dedicated to St. Peter. The legends on the first and second bells are in fine Gothic characters. There is on number 2, after the word " Nobis," the impress of the reverse of a groat of the reign of Edward III.

STANDISH (5 miles N.W. from Stroud).

The Church of St. Nicholas was formerly connected with a fraternity dedicated to the Holy Cross, consisting of 13 men. It has an imposing steeple containing six bells. The following are the legends, etc., on them :—

No. 1.—The Treble. "Charity brought me here in 1720 year."

No. 2.—Gloriam Dei in Excelsis Sono, 1656.

No. 3.—W. CHEW, G. STRATFORD, Cardi, 1656.

No. 4.—GILES WEYMAN, JOHN PRIDY, Church. Feare God, Anno 1651.

No. 5.—" Peace and Good Neighbourhood." A. R., 1748.

No. 6 or Tenor.—   Sancta : Maria : Ero Srce Vrre : Pissima Servo. Win.

The same cyphers occur on this bell as were formerly to be seen on a boss on a ceiling in Hardwicke Church.

RANDWICK (1½ miles N.W. from Stroud).

This little village, noted for its "Wap," or Lord Mayor's Show, possesses a tiny old church, which has been restored beyond recognition. Dedicated to St. John, its old tower contains four small bells in a minor key.

The Tenor is inscribed, " God prosper this parish. R. V. RUDHALL, bell-founder, 1717."

No. 2.—Mr. NATHANIEL EILES, Churchwarden, A. R., 1701.

No. 3.—Sancta Margareta + Ora Pro Nobis +

No. 4.—+ Sancta Egidii +

MINCHINHAMPTON AND EASTINGTON CHURCHES.
(IN THE STROUD VALLEY). *Photos by C. Upton and H. J. Comley.*

AVENING CHURCH. *Photo by Chas. Upton.*

CHURCH BELLS OF MID-GLOUCESTERSHIRE.

Nos. 3 and 4 are pre-Reformation bells ; No. 3 is supposed to have formerly belonged to a convent, while No. 4, dedicated to St. Giles, seems to have been very happily placed, he being the patron saint of woods and forests, and Randwick being surrounded by woods.

HARESCOMBE (3½ miles N.W. from Stroud).

The country village of Harescombe, whose little church, situate in a hollow, is dedicated to St. John the Baptist, is an ancient place. The church has a small bell turret containing two small bells, one of which was re-cast in 1883, and formerly contained this legend :—

"In honore Beate Marie Virginis."

This, of course, is a pre-Reformation bell. The other bell has no inscription.

PITCHCOMBE (2 miles N. of Stroud).

This little village has only one bell, and that an ancient one. It bears the legend :—

"Johannes Vocabitur" (He shall be called John).

PAINSWICK (3½ miles N. by E. from Stroud).

Painswick has a fine peal of twelve bells, which were restored in 1901. They have made this village famous, for their ringers have "broken the record" for change-ringing. The writer has, however, failed to discover anything further about them.

E. P. FENNEMORE.

STONEHOUSE CHURCH.

Photo by H. J. Comley.

Roman Gloucestershire: "My Favourite Walk."

I T is not because there are not a number of interesting routes to take in the district in which I live, nor because I do not desire with others to have occasionally a change, but there are so many beauties to be seen, so much pleasure to be derived in "My favourite walk," that I venture to put it before visitors to the district as follows :—

I assume that you can walk ten or fifteen miles a day, and are used to it, in which case you will know that up hill and down dale is very much better than along the level road. It develops different sets of muscles, and one can walk farther, and have finer views.

Start from Stroud early in the day, say eight or nine o'clock, walk down the canal side to Ryeford, turn off to King Stanley Church, go through the stile and make for Leonard Stanley Church, which will well repay a visit. The Norman doorway at the west end and some very interesting examples of different types of architecture will help to interest you awhile. Rest under the old yew tree in God's acre, if you like, upon the row of tombstones sacred to the memory of a family once well-known in the district, but who have long since left it, and whose name even is only a remembrance.

From there go on to "Frocester George," where you will arrive about eleven o'clock. If you are a teetotaller, good ; if not, take note, it is a "free house," with spacious rooms and an old-time air of comfort, sadly lacking in the bars of most modern palaces dedicated to "Bacchus." After resting, go to the old gateway of Frocester Court, where you will find an erection which was put up to the memory of "Good Queen Bess," who, in the course of her triumphal movements, visited this very beautiful old house, and slept there. Note the celebrated old tithe barn which was built "before the days of contracting," when trunks of trees roughly shaped were used for principals ; note, too, the solidity and strength, which, perhaps, in our modern view is too liberal for the stress, but which nevertheless please the eye, and, best of all, have stood the test of time.

Now, figuratively, gird up your loins, and, with staff in hand, go resolutely up Frocester Hill. This is one of the most lovely portions of the walk. Rising up from the plain you will gradually get a broader and more extensive view of the lovely valley of the Severn, in the distance, on your right. Notice the "silver streak" of that river, which has been traversed for æons of years by Briton, Roman and later races. If you have a field-glass, you can half-way up the hill discern the Severn Bridge in the far distance, and to the right of this, the "Sugarloaf" of Abergavenny. You will notice some distance to the left a very fine view gradually unfolded, of Stinchcombe Hill. When you get nearly to the top the hedge on the right-hand side of the road ceases, and you get a view of two curiously-shaped hills, one known as "Cam Down," but more freely described by the rural inhabitants as the "Dough Trough," and "Cam Peak," beyond. Curiously-shaped, are they not ? What does it mean ? To the reader of Donnelly's "Atlantis," it may suggest similar hills mentioned by him in Mexico. The Peak ? Well, you have heard of Silbury Hill, in Wiltshire, and you have heard of the Pyramids. Is there a connection? It is very hard to say. There may be, and I have always found it very pleasant to think that in this lovely spot, centuries ago, neolithic man may have worshipped, and, like Moses on Mount Sinai, like the Manxman at the Tynwald, before man read and wrote, Archdruids or High Priests, or leaders of men may have proclaimed the law from the top of that peak. Certain it is that vast multitudes would have been able to see the leader expounding and explaining the law, and thus bring themselves in touch with the enactments of their country, ignorance of which, even to the ignorant in those days, would have been no excuse for breaking them.

Further up the hill will be noticed, on the left, an exposure of the strata, typical oolite, which is decidedly of interest to the geologist. At the top of the hill is a finger post. Now, turn round, and " View the landscape o'er." Open your lungs, and get a full draught of God's rich, pure air, and realize what is meant when it is said " He breathed into man the breath of life." If you are poetical or comtemplative, or philosophical, and care little for the rush and din of life, preferring rather to "court solitude, so that your soul may have every chance to grow," a rest here will do you good, and besides the physical blessings accruing from your walk, you will get a spiritual uplifting, without which all walks are barren.

When you again proceed, go straight on the Uley road until you come to a cottage. Ask there for the key of the Tumulus, and as I have been, accompanied by an intelligent lad, and, having left threepence (the Government fee per head) with the cottager, go back to the Tumulus. Don't be afraid to enter, althongh it means going in on hands and knees. Get inside that mound, and, remember when you are there, that you are in a tomb which is probably four or five thousand years old.

If you can get a copy of Blunt's " Dursley and Neighbourhood," take it with you. He gives a most interesting account of the Tumulus and the district you are going to traverse. Suffice it here to say, there can be no doubt that this tomb was built by neolithic man. Skeletons, with skulls of the Iberian type, were found when the tomb was originally opened, and if you have been to similar mounds in other parts of the country, or have read any of the standard works on the subject, you will soon recognise that this is one of the most perfect remains of the " Long Barrow " type known.

Outside, look all round at the panorama, and realize how much of poetry and beauty there were in the thought of burying their dead, probably their great dead, in such a beautiful situation.

After this to other scenes. Back to the cottage giving up the key, and if you are a teetotaller, partaking of the innocuous temperance beverage sold there, then, instead of dipping down into Uley, walk on to the Bury. The mound on the right-hand side is where the gate or entrance to this old Roman camp originally stood. Bear round to the right Notice how wonderfully the situation lent itself to fortification in days when " Long Toms " were unknown. A nearer view can here be obtained of Cam Down and Cam Peak. As you go round the first turning to the left, you will see Dursley nestling in its beauty under the lee of Stinchcombe Hill. Further round, by the first of two old entrances to the camp, you get the first glimpse of Uley. From this point of view one of the prettiest villages I wot of, once a seat of the woollen industry, it has since lost a great deal, if not all of its former commercial influence. But now that the shuttle shoots no longer and the whirr of the machinery has gone, Nature has still many and greater charms to offer.

Continuing round the Bury you will come across the second of the old roads out from the Bury to other places, and about two or three hundred yards further round you will come back to where you started from, having completed in the circuit about a statute mile.

This Bury was originally the " Aldershot " of the many Roman camps in the district, the centre of a chain of forts extending from Clifton Down to Bredon Hill. Get Blunt's most interesting account into your mind, and, with the charm of the place you will be likely to remember it all.

Go down the hill from the Bury into Uley, but instead of going through that ancient village, turn to the left down Fiery Lane, asking the way to Owlpen Church. It is a pretty little isolated " Mecca," almost Irish in its bijou tininess. Ask permission of the caretaker at the house close by to see over the old Manor House. If you obtain it, and it is rarely, if ever, withheld, you will indeed have a treat. The house, with its quaint exterior and interior, carries you back in our history to the days when, so far as the upper classes at any rate were concerned, there was more gallantry, more beauty and variety of dress, and, shall we say, sunnier smiles and happier laughter than we get to-day ? If the roses are in bloom you will enjoy a rest outside more than you ordinarily would. The towering yews, the terraces, in fact everything is so delightfully old and pleasing that it is quite difficult to tear oneself away from it.

Leaving the Manor House, proceed on through the wood, where you will get some charming little bits of sylvan scenery, and where in their seasons, you

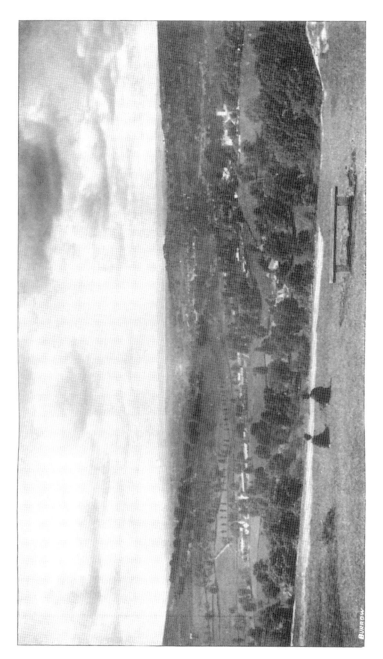

Photo. by H J. Comley.

THE SEVERN VIEW.

MY FAVOURITE WALK.

will see beautiful violets, orchids, primroses or other wild flowers, and come out on top of the range once more.

You are now on top of the Cotswolds looking east, and are at liberty to either go on through Horsley into Nailsworth, where you can take train or 'bus to Stroud, or you can come back through Nymphsfield, a beautifully quaint old village, to the old entrance of Woodchester Park, and then (if you have obtained permission) a walk down the drive, past the house into Woodchester, is a really wonderful experience. Game, all innocent of the cruel hand of man, run about in thousands quite close. You gaze upon sunny glades where browse contented kine and flocks—an infinite variety of countless trees, lakes, where occasionally big fish roll, or on which moor hens dart, the perspectives, the different views and the flowers, all are charming.

I have walked and driven through this park many times, and have always enjoyed it. Every time I go I see something fresh and beautiful, of different aspect, which lends fuller interest to what must always be the most beautiful park in this district.

THE WOODCHESTER VALLEY.   *Photo by Smith.*

After you have left the park, Woodchester Station is not far off, or if you have walked fairly briskly, and not delayed too long revelling in the beauties you have seen, the 5·30 Nailsworth 'bus will pick you up at the bottom of the hill, and bring you back to Stroud.

You will not ask me, after you have been this walk, why I selected it. But to induce you to take it, I will briefly summarize what you will see.

One of the finest remains of pre-historic man.

One of the largest Roman encampments in Gloucestershire.

A fine old church, with interesting architectural features.

Mediæval and Elizabethan houses.

Nature in her most beautiful aspect, and peaceful, smiling, English landscapes.

But above all, you will have had in your walk the benefit of inhaling some of the richest and purest air in the district. If your mind has been attuned to the scenery and associations, and is capable of receiving lasting impressions, you will not soon forget your pleasant experiences. Perchance you will desire to repeat them, in which case take a friend, and thus spread abroad the fame and the beauty of our glorious county.

JAMES HARPER.

Through Toadsmoor Valley.

ONE of the many enjoyable walks in the neighbourhood of Stroud is over the hill into Toadsmoor Valley. Whether the pedestrian be antiquarian, botanist, geologist, biologist or entomologist, he will find something of interest if he goes at a suitable season. Starting from Trinity Church, along Horn's Road, you come to the corner of Stroud Cemetery. There take the pathway on your right hand, leading into Horn's Valley and up past Weighouse, taking the road between two walls, which leads to some cottages called "Heavens." Some twenty-five years ago a stout gentleman had been directed this way to Bussage. He met a lad up the road, and asked him the name of the place just in front. "Heaven," replied the boy. Thanking him, the gentleman remarked. "How characteristic! Narrow the path, and difficult the way."

Yes, it is rather a sharp pull to get up. But it will amply repay you when there Passing by the cottages into a field, follow the pathway across to a stone stile by a large tree. But stay ; look round from this point. You will get a feast for the eyes and food for the mind. Away on the horizon on a clear day you will see the Sugar Loaf at Abergavenny and other Welsh mountains. Nearer is the Forest of Dean, with the Severn flowing like a silver streak. Nearer still are Stonehouse, Ebley and Cainscross, while the town of Stroud seems to lie almost at your feet. Slightly on the right are the villages of Randwick and Whiteshill, with a fine background of beautiful woodland. A little to the left, on a peak of Rodborough Hill, stands "The Fort," and on the eastern slope is Butterrow, while farther round is "Wall's Quarry," above which lies Minchinhampton Common, famous for its golf links, and dry, bracing air. Now we must get on, and visit the old Elizabethan residence called Mackhouse, which lies on our left. This once belonged to Charles Coxe, one of the Judges of Wales, who rebuilt it. It still contains a few remnants of antiquity.

Now follow a cart-track across the fields, which leads to Quarhouse Quarries, the stone from which was at one time thought much of and is still occasionally sought for. It has been said that George Ridler, of Gloucestershire notoriety, got the stones from here to build his oven. If so, he probably lived somewhere near. According to "Fisher" there were Ridlers here in Judge Coxe's time. Taking a look round from this eminence, we get a lovely view of the Golden Valley and places in the immediate vicinity. But we must retrace our steps to Mackhouse ; and, having arrived on the green, we turn down to the right and come to the entrance to Mackhouse Woods. Here, on the left, you will see an obelisk erected by Judge Coxe to the memory of a favourite horse. It is about twelve feet high, standing on a base of three or four feet, and on it is the following inscription :—

> "My name was Wag, that rolled the green,
> The oldest horse that ever was seen ;
> My years they numbered forty-two ;
> I served my master just and true."

A little way on our right, in the woods, you will find some caves where stone was formerly excavated. We must now turn back down the road through the wood, and decide whether we will go further or return to Stroud. If the walk has been enough, take the road to the right, which leads into the Chalford Road just below the railway station, from whence you can return by rail or 'bus. But if instead you wish to continue the walk, we will turn to the left. On the hillside at our right lies the village of Bussage ; in front of us Toadsmoor Valley, delightful at all times, bnt especially in autumn, when the trees are clothed in their richest garb. Keeping on the main road, up the side of the hill on our

THROUGH TOADSMOOR VALLEY.

right, we come into the village of Eastcombe, and from here get a lovely view of the wooded valley and Lypiatt Park, the seat of Sir J. E. Dorington, Bart., M.P. From here you can proceed to Bisley. Some people may prefer to keep in the valley ; if so, instead of going up the road to Eastcombe, turn down a lane past a few cottages. This brings us to Toadsmoor Lake. Here are fish and fowl on your right, pheasants and rabbits on your left, and overhead a concert of feathered songsters. We are now on the Lypiatt estate. Passing on we come to the woodman's house. Pause and think and, if you like, sing that old song—

"Oh, woodman, spare that tree ;
Touch not one single bough ;
In youth it sheltered me,
And I'll protect it now."

Passing on up the valley we come to Bismoor, a few cottages lying on the hillside at our right. Keeping to the cart-track, on past the keeper's house, we arrive at Bisley. If it should be a hot day, we may refresh ourselves with a draught of crystal water at the Seven Springs. On Ascension Day these are decorated with garlands by school children, who then walk in procession and have their annual tea. We must take a glance at the fine old church, and can enter the churchyard either by climbing "Jacob's Ladder," (a long flight of steps close by the springs), or by following the road to High Street, and then, turning to the left, pass through a lychgate. There is much that is ancient connected with this church, it having been the "Mother of Stroud," from which it was separated in 1304, though Stroud belonged to the parish until 1360. Passing out at the top corner by the schools, we come into the main road, and, turning to the left, make for home. About a mile out of Bisley can be seen another view of the mansion belonging to the lord of the manor, Sir John E. Dorington. Soon after passing through an avenue of sycamores we come to the main entrance to the Park. Looking about north, between here and the finger-post, on a clear day the Malvern Hills can be seen. Descending the hill, we see the old Stroud road on the right, which was formerly the highway between Stroud and London *via* Bisley. From this point there is a splendid view of the Berkeley Vale and Cotswold Peaks, with the Severn visible at several points of its serpentine course.

GEO. HOLMES.

WOODCHESTER.   *Photo by H. J. Comley.*

BURROW

Photo by H. J. Comley.

TOADSMOOR LAKE.

Riding, Driving, and Cycling Routes in the Stroud District.

See Map on Page 35.

S a centre for a series of charming cycling runs, Stroud cannot be beaten. At all points of the compass there is a wealth of scenery unsurpassed in beauty, with a profusion of Roman antiquities, old churches, castles, and "stately homes," making the district particularly interesting to those who are at all fond of wandering among the reminders of an ancient past. The Cotswolds have a great advantage—from a cyclist's standpoint—over most hill ranges, in that there are many excellent cycling roads on them, extending in some cases to the outer spurs of the hills, and keeping from 500 to 700 ft., or more, above sea level. It is in taking trips on these "highroads" that one learns to fully appreciate the charm of the Cotswolds.

Nature has been very lavish in the neighbourhood in her display of hill and dale, wood and water, the various valleys radiating from Stroud being at all times full of beauty, the most delightful time, perhaps, being in the month of June, when the wealth of roses—for which the cottage gardens of this part are famous—is a sight not easily forgotten. The cyclist who has not yet explored this part of the county has certainly missed one of the most beautiful corners of England.

ROUTE I.

Frocester, Uley Bury, Beverstone Castle, Tetbury, Malmesbury.

Through Cainscross to Ryeford, over the Stroudwater Canal, and through the beautiful avenue to King's Stanley—where the Kings of Mercia resided—then on to Leonard Stanley, or, to give it its old name, Stanley St. Leonard's, where you see the fine Norman Church and thatched cottages. A very pleasant run of about a mile brings you to Frocester (4½ miles).

Frocester Court was visited by Queen Elizabeth in 1574, on her way to Berkeley Castle; over the porch is the bedroom occupied by her during her visit; close by is the massive old tithe-barn—erected about 1300—the largest remaining in England. You will now have a climb up the well-engineered road to the top of Frocester Hill, where you will be rewarded with a magnificent view of the Severn Valley, and, if it is clear, of the hills of Malvern and South Wales. Taking the Uley Road, a ride of ½ mile brings you in sight of the famous Uley Tumulus (dealt with in another part of this volume), which lies about 200 yards to the right of the road. Another ½ mile, and you will be in the Roman camp on Uley Bury (7½ miles), which occupies a very commanding position, and called by Blunt, the local historian, "The Roman Aldershot." Returning to top of Frocester Hill, proceed on the Bath Road, passing Nymphsfield—an old weaving village—and Owlpen. Coming to Kingscote, take the Tetbury Road to Calcut Barn (13 miles), a fine structure, with a Roman altar stone built in the wall; then on to Beverstone (14½ miles), with its interesting old castle, not nearly so well known as it ought to be. (A capital history of the castle is given by Blunt in his history of Dursley and neighbourhood). A run of 2 miles more, and you are in Tetbury (16½ miles), where see the quaint old market-house, and the church, with its beautiful clerestoried nave. (If you have time, it is well worth your while to take the 5-mile run from here to Malmesbury, inspecting there the fine old Abbey, with its magnificent Norman doorway, one of the finest in England). Leaving Tetbury by the Avening road, a short detour will bring you to Chavenage House, an Elizabethan mansion, said to have been occupied by the three Republican generals—Cromwell, Lord Essex and Ireton. A short pleasant run, and you will drop into Avening (21 miles), where see the remarkable Norman church; then on through the ever-lovely Avening Valley to Nailsworth, and from there to Woodchester, where there are some beautiful remains of Roman tesselated pavement, under a portion of the old churchyard—

CHALFORD, NEAR STROUD.   *Photo by Dr. Garrett.*

pity 'tis that they cannot have a suitable roof put over them! This pavement is described by Canon Lysons, as " Superior for size and richness to any found in Britain, and excelled by few in any of the Roman Provinces." Woodchester also possesses a Dominican Priory and a Franciscan Convent. From here a run of rather more than 2 miles brings you into Stroud. A very delightful alternative run home from Avening may be had by taking the upper road through Minchinhampton, over the bracing common of golf fame, and calling at Amberley—the Enderley of John Halifax, Gentleman—to see the famous Rose Cottage, where the book was written; then riding along to Rodboro' Fort for the fine view from there, and down the hill to Stroud, thus keeping on high ground for the greater part of the trip.

Total distance about 28 miles.
Including Malmesbury, about 38 miles.

ROUTE II.

Eastington, Berkeley, Sharpness and Framilode.

Leave Stroud *via* Cainscross, and along the Bristol road, leaving Stonehouse, to the right. Near the Midland Station, on the left, is Stonehouse Court, visited by Queen Elizabeth, who stopped one night there. Near the court is the Parish Church—quite a good walk from the village, where George Whitfield, the famous preacher, was curate in 1736, preaching his first open-air sermon in the churchyard there, the congregation being too large for the church. A pleasant run of about a mile, and you cross the Stroudwater canal, passing through Eastington (5 miles), after which a short run brings you into the Land's End to John O'Groat's Road (take left), which affords capital running through Cambridge and Berkeley Road to Berkeley Heath, and the Old Bell Inn, where

MARKET DAY AT CIRENCESTER, NEAR STROUD. *Photo by Dr. Garrett.*

the merry Pickwick Party stayed for lunch on their way from Bristol to Birmingham (you will find a copy of the Pickwick Papers inside). Take the road to right for Berkeley (13½ miles). The charming old castle—where Edward II. was murdered in 1307—is the oldest inhabited castle in England, and is, by the kindness of Lord Fitzhardinge, open to the public on Mondays, Wednesdays and Thursdays, from 10 o'clock to 4. It has been held continuously by the same family—with one short break—from 1154 to the present day. The church is well worth close inspection ; in the west door there are striking traces—in the shape of bullet marks, and slits for muskets—of the castle siege in 1645, when the church, which was occupied by part of the garrison, was taken by the

Parliamentarians. Two very quaint epitaphs may be seen on tombs in the churchyard. Dr. Jenner, the introducer of vaccination, was born at Berkeley, and lived and died there, being buried in the family vault at east end of chancel ; a beautiful memorial to him may be seen in the great east window. A run of about 2 miles brings you to Sharpness, where the fine docks, and the entrance to the Gloucester Ship Canal — 16 miles without a lock — will well repay inspection. The return to the Gloucester Road may be made by a short cut *via* Moorend and Slimbridge, the latter place being interesting as providing £10 yearly out of the church living for a musical commemoration of the College of St. Mary Magdalen, Oxford, a Latin hymn being sung at 5 a.m., on the 1st of May annually, on the top of Magdalen College Tower. A run of about 2 miles more up the Gloucester road, and you are at the turning (left) for Frampton. Ride round the splendid village green, one of the finest in England. There is a remarkably quaint epitaph on a stone in the churchyard—near the chancel—to a former sexton and his six wives. Another short run (left on leaving the green), and you are close by the beautiful church at Fretherne, built at great cost by the late Rev. Sir Wm. Lionel Darell, Bart., who was rector of the parish for 34 years. Fretherne Court, a very fine mansion, the residence of Sir Lionel Darell, Bart., is near the church. Taking the road to the right, opposite the church, a ride of 1¼ miles brings you to Framilode, the local watering-place. With the tide fully in, the Severn is really magnificent here, and it is a charming sight, and one not readily forgotten, to watch, under the light of the moon, the Severn bore tearing its way up the river, the accompanying roar being most striking at this quiet spot. A very pleasant ride through Saul, over the ship and Stroud-water canals—passing several well-known nightingale groves, where Philomel discourses her delightful cadenzas during her too brief stay—and you arrive at Whitminster Church—some distance from the village—which is well worth a visit. Passing on through Whitminster (crossing the Gloucester Road) and Nupend, you soon complete the circle, and a run of about 4½ miles brings you home again.

Total distance about 33 miles.

ROUTE III.

Painswick, Birdlip, Cirencester, Bibury, Fairford.

Start through Beeches Green to Painswick, where see the church and churchyard, the feature of the latter being the numerous clipped yew trees. Close by the stocks may still be seen. A short but rather hard ride brings you to the Adam and Eve Inn, where leave your machine and climb the hill, which

IN FRAMPTON VILLAGE.   *Photo by Dr. Garrett.*

is crowned with a very fine British camp still in a capital state of preservation. The Romans also made use of this camp, Roman coins having been found there ; and it was also held by the troops of Charles I. during the Civil War. It commands a magnificent view of the Severn valley. being over 900 feet above sea level. Leaving the Adam and Eve, a short run brings you to Halls in the Wood, where at fork in road take the right, going through the beautiful Cranham Woods to Birdlip (9 miles). This is one of the vantage grounds of the Cotswolds, the views being extremely fine, the grand range of the Malvern hills being very striking from this point. The Roman Ermine Way to Gloucester, as straight as though ruled with a ruler for nearly seven miles, with the city and Cathedral as a finish, is also a very striking feature. (There are remains of a Roman villa at Witcombe, about two miles from Birdlip, going towards Gloucester.) From Birdlip to Cirencester you traverse the Roman Ermine Way, a typical Roman road. Cirencester (19 miles), the Roman Corinium, is the junction of the four Roman highways—the Ermine Way, the Fosse Way, Akeman Street and Icknield Street—and, judging by the remains found there, it must have been a place of great importance during the Roman occupation.

The grand Abbey Church, the magnificent Park (where the poet Pope was wont to wander), by the kindness of the Earl of Bathurst always open to the public (though not to bicycles) ; these and the Museum, with its collection of Roman antiquities discovered in the district, will give you a chance of varying the day's exercise.

Before returning homewards—if time will allow—you would do well to take the round through Barnsley to Bibury, the latter surely the bonniest village in England. Near Bibury, to westward, is the little village of Ablington, in whose manor house lived Mr. J. Arthur Gibbs, the genial author of that delightful book '' A Cotswold Village,'' and whose early death everyone who has read the book must deeply deplore. From Bibury go through Colne St. Aldwyns—another charming village, where the present Chancellor of the Exchequer, Sir Michael Hicks Beach, owns and occupies the fine old manor house—and Quarnington on to Fairford (31½ miles), with its famous church and sixteenth century painted windows. These windows were taken out and hidden away during the Civil Wars, or they might have shared the fate of many others. A pleasant run of eight miles through Poulton and Ampney Crucis—where see the church and fourteenth century cross in the churchyard—brings you back to Cirencester (39½ miles), where take the Stroud road, passing (on your left) the Royal Agricultural College, which attracts pupils from all over the world, and on over the Sapperton Tunnel and down the hill, passing picturesque Chalford, so charmingly set on the hillside at the entrance to the Golden Valley, and then through bustling Brimscombe home.

Total distance, about 51 miles.

ROUTE IV.

Brookthorpe, Glo'ster, Cheltenham, Tewkesbury and Deerhurst.

Leaving Stroud by Beeches Green, you take the road up the hill to Pitchcombe, through Horsepools, and down the hill to Brookthorpe, where see the quaint thirteenth century church of St. Swithin. Passing through the fine avenue of elms at Whaddon, you soon reach the county town (8½ miles). Here, of course the first objective is the grand old Cathedral, which will absorb a large portion of the cyclist's day if it is examined as it deserves. Other interesting sights not to be missed are Bishop Hooper's Monument, near the Cathedral ; the delightfully quaint New Inn, built for the use of the pilgrims to the shrine of Edward II. about 1455 ; and Robert Raikes' house in Southgate Street. This list is very incomplete, but you have other country ahead, so, leaving the city by Northgate Street, you proceed to take the pleasant 8½-mile run to Cheltenham. The fine Promenade, with its beautiful trees, claims—and usually gets—first attention here. Cheltenham College, Pittville Park and various waters (which neither cheer nor inebriate) will keep you occupied for some time here. Take the Tewksbury road, *via* High Street and Coombe Hill, usually a capital surface, giving excellent running to Tewkesbury (25 miles). The splendid Abbey Church, full of historic interest ; the Bell Hotel, close by, where Phineas Fletcher, of " John Halifax " fame, resided ; the Hop Pole, of Pickwickian interest ; the fine timbered houses, reminiscent of Chester ; the junction of the Avon and Severn—these will keep you fully interested. Leaving the town by the Gloucester road (the one you entered by), you pass the famous battlefield where the rival York and Lancastrian forces fought the decisive battle of 1471. About 2½ miles down the road take the right turn for Deerhurst (which lies about two miles from the main road), to see the interesting Saxon church and curious ninth-century font, and the small Saxon chapel near the church, discovered in 1884. Returning to the Gloucester road, you will have very good surface, through charming country, into the city, which leave by Southgate Street ; passing near to Hempstead on the right (fine old church and cross) ; leaving Stonebench, also on the right (the best place to see the Severn " bore "), and going through Quedgley, Hardwicke, Standish and Stonehouse home— a " truly rural " run.

Total distance, about 51 miles.

TEWKESBURY FROM THE MEADOWS.

ROUTE V.

Tetbury, Weston Birt, Badminton, Tortworth and Dursley.

Leave Stroud by London road, turning right at Bowbridge, up Butterrow, and over Minchinhampton Common (presented to the parish by Dame Alice Hampton in the reign of Henry VIII.) Then on through Minchinhampton, Avening and Tetbury (see Route I.) to Weston Birt (12½ miles), famous for the beautiful gardens of Weston Birt House (the residence of Captain Holford), undoubtedly one of the finest show places in the county. The grounds and gardens are simply magnificent. See also the old church in the grounds, with the beautiful monument to the late Squire Holford. Take the Bath road on leaving here, going through the pretty village of Didmarton (in which parish the Avon rises), after leaving which you are soon at Badminton (18½ miles— a household word among sporting men, the stately home of the Duke of Beaufort. See the fine park here, with its magnificent beech avenue nearly three miles long, and the church with the fine monuments to members of the Beaufort family. Lord Raglan, who commanded the English forces in the Crimea, and who died there, was buried here in 1855. The stables and kennels are also well worth inspection.

Leave Badminton by the Hawkesbury Upton road, near to which place is a very fine tower erected in 1846 to General Lord Robert Somerset. From this point you get a very extensive and charming view of the south-western portion of the county.

A very pleasant run down the hill, through Hillesley and Alderley, brings you to Wotton-under-Edge (26 miles). See the church here and the ancient chapel of St. Katharine. The old town of Wotton was burnt out in the reign of King John. (If time will allow, you will do well to take the trip from here through Charfield to Tortworth (4½ miles), to see the seat of the Earl of Ducie and the famous old chesnut tree near the church—so old that it was known as the "great chestnut of Tortworth" in King Stephen's time.)

Take the road from here (somewhat up and down) to North Nibley, where William Tyndale, the first translator of the Bible, was born in 1484. A very striking monument to the Gloucestershire martyr is erected on Nibley Knoll, and is quite a landmark in the district.

The road from here by Stinchcombe to Dursley is of a "switchbacky" character, but the trouble involved is more than repaid by the delightful nature of the scenery. Dursley (32 miles) is a very quaint old town, and at one time was a very important woollen manufacturing place. See the splendid old church and the Town Hall and Market House, with the statue of Queen Anne. A pleasant run through Upper Cam (see the fine old church of St. George), Lower Cam, Coaley and Frocester (see Route I.), and you are soon on the main road to Stroud and home.

Total distance, about 41 miles.

Including Tortworth, about 50 miles.

J. R. PEARSON.

THE PROMENADE, CHELTENHAM (from Stroud, 14 miles).

Photo by Smith.

THE GOLDEN VALLEY, CHALFORD.

The Golden Valley.

THE picturesque village of Chalford, which is large
and populous and is situated in a valley of singular
beauty, may be reached either on foot or on the
omnibus, which runs hourly from the end of
Russell Street, Stroud. The distance is about
four miles and the fare threepence. Many persons
go there and back on the top of the omnibus for
the sake of the scenery and the air. The road
follows the line of the valley all the way, with
Stroud Hill, Horn's Valley, Thrupp, Quarhouse,
Toadsmoor Bottom, the Bourne and Brown's Hill
on the left, and the river Froom, the canal and
the Great Western Railway on the right, flanked
by the high range of Rodborough and Minchinhampton Commons. On this latter common are
the famous golf links and the village of Amberley,
where the air is said to be as fine as anywhere in England.

The story of the formation of this road is interesting. Down
to 1814 the road from Stroud to Chalford was a curious switchback
along the broken hillside to the left of the present road. You can still take this
route if you prefer it. Passing up the middle of the town, it took a steep descent
to Bowbridge, turned sharply up the hillside again to Thrupp, and, giving by
the way many a lovely view, descended into Toadsmoor Bottom at the Bourne.
Thence it climbed the hillside anew, and, passing through Blacknest and Brown's
Hill, it ran down Skate's Hill into Chalford. It required a whole day for a
team of horses to drag a loaded waggon from Stroud to Chalford and to return,
although the distance is only four miles in a straight line. The turnpike road
to Cirencester and London lay at that time along the summit of Rodborough
Hill, on the opposite side of the valley, and, besides being steeper and longer,
was useless for communication between Stroud and Chalford. In 1814 an Act
was obtained for making a new road. There was opposition to the plan but
the Commissioners assembled a large body of labourers, who commenced opera-
tions in the night, and had levelled the hedges and other obstructions on a considerable portion of the intended road before the mill-owners and others arose
in the morning, and before any contracts had been made for the land over
which it was to pass. This invaluable highway was opened in 1815, the year of
the Battle of Waterloo.

Starting, then, along this road, Rodborough Fort (or Fort St. George, to
call it by its correct name), on the wooded hill to the right, marks conspicuously
the end of Rodborough Common. That elevated point commands one of the
most magnificent views in the neighbourhood. The panorama stretches to the
Severn (eight miles away) and to the oak-covered hills of the Forest of Dean
beyond, and when the atmosphere is clear the Sugar Loaf mountain at Abergavenny and the Black mountains of Herefordshire are plainly visible forty
miles away. But we are in the valley, and, as a tired friend of mine once said,
"The hills look very well from below."

Passing Capel's Mill and Arundel's Mill on the little river Froom to the
right, through the village of Bowbridge (so called from its bowed bridge over the
canal), and pausing a moment to notice its dye-houses and the quaint village of
Butterrow winding up the steep hillside, we come to Thrupp, with its thatched
iron church, a village which, from its base of mills by the water, rises up the
steep hillside to the left, and is capped by an extensive wood—the Park Wood.
The upper part of the village is in two clusters—Near Thrupp and Far Thrupp.
so called in reference to their distance from Stroud. There is a good Board

Photo by H. J. Comley.

THE LOCK AT CHALFORD.

THE GOLDEN VALLEY.

School in Far Thrupp, and a rope-walk along the hillside, with its rustic sheds, forms a picturesque feature.

Thrupp in Icelandic means a hill, and in Danish a village. Both meanings are descriptive of the place.

In the principal house, which is called "The Thrupp," lived William Henry Stanton, who was member of Parliament for Stroud from 1841 to 1852. He and his nephews were the owners of Stafford's Mill, which we have passed on the road, and which was formerly the scene of one of the best cloth businesses of the neighbourhood.

Griffin's Mill, so named from the family who owned it before the year 1600, and held it for two hundred years, comes next. It is now used as a stick mill. Ham Mill, formerly a flourishing cloth mill, now a carpet factory, is of equally ancient origin. It was twice destroyed by fire, in 1841 and 1866.

During the period of the Civil War the wealthy clothiers of this district, who had much business with the woolstaplers of Cirencester and the merchants of Bristol, obtained from Prince Maurice and his brother Prince Rupert letters of protection against the military in these places. The originals of two of these letters, granted to Samuel Webb, of Stroudwater, clothier, are still in the possession of Sir J. E. Dorington, of Lypiatt Park, near by.

Passing Phœnix Iron Foundry by the canal on the right, and noticing all the way the lovely bays and promontories of the wooded hills, we reach the village of Brimscombe. On the right-hand side of the road is an ancient house, formerly called Bigg's Place, with extensive cloth mills adjoining. It was the property of William Dallaway, an eminent clothier and High Sheriff of the county, who died in 1776. His nephew, the Rev. James Dallaway, was a notable man. He was curate of Rodborough, chaplain and physician to the Embassy at Constantinople under Lord Bute, and afterwards librarian to the Duke of Norfolk. He was the author of several works, amongst which were "The Origin and Progress of Heraldry in England," 1793; "Constantinople, Ancient and Modern," 1797; "Lady Mary Wortley Montagu's Letters," 1803; "Anecdotes of the Arts in England," 1800; "Horace Walpole's Anecdotes of Painting in England"; "Discourses on Architecture," 1806; and "Antiquities of Bristol." The principal business at Brimscombe is the manufacture of cloth by the Messrs. Evans.

We now come to the Bourne, a village at the entrance to the beautiful Toadsmoor Valley, which here branches off to the left. Bourne Mill, belonging to Messrs. Grist & Co., lies below the level of the road, and the Brimscombe Station of the Great Western Railway is on the opposite side.

The village of Bourne stretches along the hillside above us to the left. On the opposite side of the valley a bridle-path leads up the hill to Minchinhampton Common.

We are now approaching the village of Chalford. An instance of thrifty adaptation meets us almost at the entrance of the village. A large silk mill, after standing for some time empty, has been converted into dwelling-houses. The ground floor forms one set of houses, and is approached from the front; and the upper floor, which forms the other set, is approached from the back, where the ground is on a level with the first floor of the mill building.

The valley here narrows, and the main road, after passing Chalford Church, crosses the Froom, the canal and the railway, and ascends Cowcombe Hill on the right on the way to Cirencester and London.

Chalford occupies the valley and the hillside to the left of the stream. It is almost Swiss in its picturesqueness. Zigzag footpaths lead to dwellings perched wherever they can find a hold on the steep brae, and some are so inserted in the hillside that you "ascend to the lower storey and descend to the upper." Coals are carried to the cottages in panniers on donkeys' backs.

The view towards Stroud from the upper paths of this village is singularly beautiful. When you have ascended through France Lynch and Chalford Lynch, you are on the high tableland of the Cotteswold range. Lynch is Saxon for ledge, and well describes the position of the houses. The name "France" is a relic of the immigration of French Huguenots, who, flying from persecution in their own country, brought their clothing industry with them in the seventeenth century. The name "Chalford," spelt in an old deed "Chalkford," describes the position of the lower and original part of the village near a ford on the river. The oldest place of worship is the "Dissenting Meeting-house" at France, which dates from 1662, the year of the Act of Uniformity, but secret meetings for worship were held before that time by the Huguenots. The church was built in 1725. Chalford Tabernacle, with its schoolroom where the British School is carried on, is a flourishing place of worship belonging to the Baptists; and there are chapels belonging to the Wesleyans, the Primitive Methodists and the Brethren. The church at France Lynch is a chapel of ease from Bisley.

Roger Bacon, the famous Franciscan friar, was born in 1214 at Toadsmoor, and was educated at St. Mary's Chapel, Chalford. He was one of the most learned men of his day, and his experiments in mathematics, mechanics and optics caused him to be suspected of magic. He anticipated many subsequent inventions, and is credited with the discovery of gunpowder.

Chalford Waterworks, which supply good water to the whole Stroud district (being pumped up to a reservoir on Minchinhampton Common and thence distributed), occupy the beautiful valley just beyond the village, and are fed by the "hundred springs" which flow from the freestone formation of the abrupt and rocky hill on the Minchinhampton side of the valley. The beauty of this upper part of the valley in its winding course above the village has earned for it the title of the "Golden Valley," a name said to have been given to it by Queen Victoria when, in the earlier part of her reign, she passed through it on the railway. It is indeed beautiful, with its thickets, opening glades and green dells and dingles, while in the autumn it is all aglow with the bright golden tints of its beech trees.

C. A. DAVIS.

The Severn Bore.

ONCE had the pleasure of witnessing the Severn Bore on a July evening at Framilode, where the winding river broadens out, and where the bore may be seen in its best and most characteristic aspects. A muffled roar away in the south gave timely warning of its approach, and within a few minutes could be discerned a disturbance of the stream away below Severn view. On it sped in a surging torrent like a moving volume of liquid steel; back it drove the garbage of the sands and of the mud banks away up the higher reaches of the stream; on it churned with a velocity which struck the gondolas riding at anchor in the suddenly-agitated river, causing them to rear and plunge, and roll and strain at the painters which held them captive; on it came with savage force, swirling into the crevices in the broad banks which had been excavated by the recurrent tides of the previous months; on it came, churning and gurgling, hissing and dashing its spray over the edge of the banks, its grotesque patches of drab spume seeming to be engaged in a frantic race for some invisible goal; on it came in still increasing volume until, in a very few minutes, the stretch of sand which for some hours had been parching under a torrid sun, became submerged and driven up with the inexorable current, only to be ultimately swept back again seawards, and to settle in some fresh haven until it again pursued its restless course of eternal disturbance. So the tide rose with billows in its centre and serpentine swirls against the banks, until the neap was reached and the stream had exhausted the mad fury of its flow. It was impossible to watch the rising river from the bank without reflecting on the marvellous works of Nature. Those of us who now see the bore of a July evening could form some notion of its terrible and thrilling grandeur in the chill October months, when wanton gales rise and the high spring tides come with savage force and flood the river trough with a boiling and an awe-inspiring torrent.

T. H. BARROW.

No. 17 GREEN, MINCHINHAMPTON GOLF LINKS.   *Photo by H. J. Comley.*

THE SEVERN BORE.   *Photo by Joyner.*

Minchinhampton Golf Links.

NO golfer should be in Gloucestershire without playing on the Minchinhampton Links. Every Gloucestershire man is proud of these same links. He can combine romance with the game "honourable and ancient;" and, strange to say, he can be truthful! He can say, for instance, that the golf thereat is at its oldest and best in the county, so far as play and the natural aptitude of the course for the game are concerned, He can go on to say that it is the "Enderley" flat of "John Halifax, Gentleman;" that it is 700 feet and more above sea, and that it is a level plateau where scenery, health and golf are beautifully intermixed.

Golf experts pronounce the course as one of the best inland in England. The soil is not sandy, nor has it the advantages of the sea-side. But its turf is many hundred years old—springy, rich, beautiful.

I have played on some of the famous links in England and Scotland. Yet I have no hesitation in saying that there have been times when Minchinhampton can compare with the best of them. It is an 18-hole course—full of variety, and calling for many strokes—and usually many clubs!

A few particulars will not be out of place :—

No. 1. Is so arranged as kindly to allow for a practice shot or two. No difficulties, unless wilfully made.

No. 2. Drive as you like—far and sure, pull or slice, but beware of your second. Iron club, ranging from cleek to mashie, "be up," but don't go too far, else the churchyard may witness the burial of your hopes.

No. 3. The Amberley Quarry, known locally as the "Amberley Quar." Huge, ugly, gaping. This time woe betide pull or slice! Be up and over, or heart-breaking, stone-breaking!

No. 4. The point at this hole is the iron-cleek or mashie for the approach. A man's shot. Topping means trouble, and shortness spells sorrow. Be up, and with luck you are out in one more, or else your medal-round is no more.

No. 5. Don't count your chickens before they are hatched. A good drive, a large second or short second, and over with your third.

No. 6. There is not a golfer in the West of England but knows the Lomb's Hole. So simple, so natural, done in 2—and "I gies up."

Passing by others we come to the gate quarry, only an iron shot—but woe betide the long and short here ; and who is there who has not been short, or, to his grief, has not gone too far? A brave hole, just asking for a golfer's shot—"A wrest shot, wi' the cleek or iron, mon !"

Done in 1 more than once. A parting friend, an enthusiastic golfer, holds the record here ; holed out in 81—and he did it.

The Crant Quarry. You need a straight drive for your first and second. Big 'uns. Drive your farthest, lucky you, if up in 2.

Enough has been said to show the great variety of strokes required in this course.

This much can be said. It is a big driving course. The lies are good, and the greens are excellent.

It has been the scene of many encounters—Taylor and Hugh Kirkaldy, Toogood and Herd, and Brown and Fowler. Toogood, one time the professional, easily holds the record.

The club can boast of many good players, and, when putting its best team on the ground, they take a good deal of beating.

There are an excellent club-house and very good quarters at the Old Lodge. Mr. E. Boughton caters well for all visitors. The secretary, Mr. J. T. Woolwright, will gladly give any necessary information.

There is a separate course for ladies as well as a separate club. Their enthusiasm and their matches are much to be admired.

E. H. HAWKINS, M.A.

Amberley Common as a Health Resort.

UCH a nice, nice place on the slope of Enderley Hill. . . . . Did you never hear of Enderley Flat, the highest tableland in England? Such a fresh, free breezy spot—how the wind sweeps over it! I can feel it on my face still."—" John Halifax."

There are few people in this neighbourhood who will not recognise the above description of Miss Muloch's as referring to Amberley Common; and surely a more picturesque spot and more health-giving breezes it would be difficult to find.

Medical men speak in highest praise of its pure dry air, and of the suitability of the Common as a residence for people suffering from lung troubles or chronic gastric disturbances, whilst as a pick-me-up after brain-fag and overwork it is equal to any seaside resort. The heat of summer is rendered bearable by an invigorating breeze blowing more or less from the Bristol Channel. In winter the absence of the dense fog which prevails in the valley makes a residence there wholesome and desirable.

The Common forms the summit of one of the most beautiful tablelands in England, covering over a thousand acres, and standing at an elevation of about 700 feet above the sea level amidst the peaks and spurs of the Cotswolds— " a broad green sweep, nothing but sky and common, common and sky "— surrounded by most lovely and varied scenery.

Amberley stands on the verge of the hill, and all round the high flat the valley lies like a moat.

Standing on the terrace, in close proximity to " Rose Cottage " (where the gifted authoress composed "John Halifax"), we gaze on a magnificent panorama, The Common here drops abruptly into the pretty valley dividing it from Wood-chester, which covers the opposite hillside, and is the home of the Dominican Monks Through the tall poplars we see rising the turrets and towers of the Monastery, surrounded on all sides by gentlemen's seats and pretty cottages perched eerie-wise amongst the surrounding clumps of woodland, whilst far away to the west rise the " everlasting hills."

Remounting the hill, the springy turf invites our tread, whilst the hum of insects and the song of birds form a pleasant accompaniment to our rambles.

We may skirt the golf links in the direction of the old-world town of Min-chinhampton, where the quaint old Market House and the church with its beautiful rose window will amply repay us for a visit.

Should we be more lazily inclined, we may fling ourselves on the sweet short grass and take our fill of the beauties of creation as exhibited in the Nailsworth Valley. Now and again we may catch a glimmer of the lakes, which repose in different altitudes, through the richly-wooded course of Woodchester Park.

It matters little in which direction we turn our steps, the scenery is ravishingly beautiful.

The Horsley Vale, the Brimscombe Valley with its numberless gorges, the Stroud Valley with its busy hive of industry, or the Vale of the Severn, alike rivalling each other in points of beauty and interest—

" Sweet intercourse
Of hill, valley, rivers, woods and plain."

Wandering through Littleworth and Houndsley, and gaining Rodborough Common, we reach The Fort. And here we have another glorious panorama.

The hill descends abruptly, and in the foreground stretches a broad fertile plain, rich in shades and dotted over with the quaint-gabled houses of the Tudor period; through the midst glides the Severn, sparkling like quicksilver beneath the kiss of the setting sun.

Photo by H. J. Conley.

AMBERLEY COMMON.

AMBERLEY COMMON AS A HEALTH RESORT.

ROSE COTTAGE, AMBERLEY, Where 'John Halifax' was written. *Photo by Smith.*

For tired mothers and little children the Common is simply ideal. Visitors need not trouble about impedimenta. The children can take donkey rides, or tumble about at their own sweet will, and gain those rosy cheeks and healthy appetites so essential to their development; and children of larger growth cannot spend much time in this spot, so delightfully removed from the "madding crowd," without feeling with Browning—

"God's in His Heaven,
All's right with the world."

Geologists will find much to interest them, likewise the botanist, whilst Woodchester holds a tempting feast to the antiquary. Cyclists will also find splendid roads to Cirencester, Tetbury, Malmesbury, Gloucester, etc.

G.W.R. : Nearest station, Stroud, 3 miles.

M.R.: Nearest station, Woodchester, 1 mile.

Mrs. JOHN WHITE, Stroud.

AT NAILSWORTH   *Photo by H. J. Comley.*

NAILSWORTH FROM WATLEDGE HILL. *Photo by Paul Smith.*

NAILSWORTH. *Photo by Smith.*

Nailsworth.

By C. W. JONES.

NAILSWORTH is situated in a lovely valley about four miles from Stroud, and from the periodical returns of the Medical Officer of Health, is a particularly healthy town. Its station being the terminus of the Midland Railway Company's Stonehouse and Nailsworth Branch makes it a centre of some importance for the surrounding district.

Golfers should carefully note that Nailsworth is the nearest railway station to the celebrated Links on Minchinhampton Common, and if on alighting they are not afraid of a slight mountaineering effort, a climb of from ten to fifteen minutes' duration, will land them at "The Old Lodge," the headquarters of the Minchinhampton Club. Those preferring to make the ascent easily and luxuriously had better telephone or drop a line to the "George" or "Railway Hotel" for a conveyance, and unless they smoke too much on the way will then arrive on the Links with a good nerve and eye, ready to encounter "Colonel Bogey" or any other doughty antagonist. The drive, by way of the zig-zag road, known as "the W" will reveal some beautiful scenery : Avening Valley stretching away in one direction and Horsley in the other, the road to the latter place gradually rising until it is lost in the Kingscote Woods.

Historically, Nailsworth dates from A.D. 740, when Athelbald, King of Mercia, granted Woodland and three estates in Woodchester and district as far as "Neglesleag" (Nailsworth) to the then Bishop of Worcester with the idea of purchasing an entrance to the Eternal Kingdoms of Heaven !

The name Nailsworth appears to have been derived from "Nagel" (a weight for wool) and "leag" (pasture or wood) ; thus "Nageleag" (wool pasture or wood). The latter part of the word was subsequently changed to "wert" (market or place) ; thus "Nagelwert" (wool market). It does not appear when the change was made, but doubtless it came about through the introduction of the cloth trade, which took place in the reign of Edward III. Fosbrooke says : "I am informed that a prime Dutch cloth-maker in Gloucestershire, had the surname of Webb given him by Edward III." He was probably an ancestor of the Webb who carried on cloth-manufacturing in Nailsworth for many years, in mills just outside the town and known to-day as "Egypt," this name having been given it in honour of one "Pharaoh" Webb.

Occupiers of mills now-a-days may well sigh for "the good old times," for the records show, that in 1175 these mills were rented at forty-four shillings per year ! Cloth manufacturing seems to have been the staple industry for a very long period, large mills being built between 1700 and 1800, and although it has not a monopoly to-day, there is still, at least, one important cloth mill (Longfords). Other notable industries now are hosiery, umbrella furniture, leather board, rugs, sticks, brewing and bacon curing. The town is governed by an Urban District Council (formed in 1894) which meets the first Tuesday in every month. Petty Sessions are held on alternate Thursdays, and there is a monthly Cattle Market.

In addition to trains, there is a good 'bus service between Nailsworth and Stroud, so that it may be considered fairly get-at-able, and this is proved by the fact that many professional and commercial gentlemen from Gloucester make its neighbourhood their place of residence.

As a centre for driving, motoring, cycling, or walking tours it has strong grounds for consideration, being situated in the midst of some of the loveliest scenery in England.

Woodchester Park (one of singular and changing beauty), Minchinhampton Common (with its unsurpassable views and Golf Links), Avening (with its charming valley), Beverston Castle (of historic fame), Frocester Hill and Kingscote (the site of an old Roman Station), are all within the reach of a good pedestrian, whilst cyclists and drivers will easily negotiate the distance to Badminton, Cirencester, Tetbury, Weston Birt, and Malmesbury, all places of great interest. For motoring we need only say that Nailsworth is on the high road to Bristol, as well as Gloucester and Bath.

Sportsmen will be glad to know that the Meets of the Badminton Foxhounds are mostly within easy reach, and a day or two weekly can be obtained with the Berkeley pack. Otters have been recently killed in the local waters, and jack and trout fishing are obtainable.   C. W. JONES.

LONGFORDS LAKE, NEAR NAILSWORTH. *Photo by Paul L. Smith.*

A COUNTRY ROAD NEAR NAILSWORTH. *Photo by Paul L. Smith.*

Woodchester Priory.

PERHAPS the most imposing religious building in the Stroud district is the Dominican Priory at Woodchester, about three miles from Stroud, on the road to Nailsworth. Erected about half a century ago, it was dedicated to the Annunciation, and the brotherhood numbers about twenty-five. Close to the priory is a mission church, erected by the late Mr. William Leigh, of Woodchester Park, at a cost of £9,000. A fine building constructed of stone, it consists of chancel, nave, aisles, chapel (or chantry), and turret, with spire 120 ft. high (containing three bells). Throughout, the building is elaborately decorated. Fine examples of carving are to be found in the high altar, the reredos, and the screen. Some magnificent examples of stained-glass windows are here to be seen. A large painting of "The Last Judgment," by Henry Doyle, occupies a position over the chancel arch. The building also contains a tomb of alabaster, with recumbent effigy to the founder, the late Mr. William Leigh, and a stone effigy to commemorate Archbishop Nicholson, bishop of Corfu, who, dying whilst on a visit to Mr. Leigh, was interred in the church. Round the walls of the aisles are fourteen carved groups representing the stations of the Cross. The Prior is the Very Rev. Vincent McNabb, S.I.L., and the sub-prior the Rev. Gabriel Whitacre. Adjoining stands the Franciscan Convent of the Immaculate Conception (founded 1859), the sisterhood comprising twenty-eight members, including an abbess. Gytha, wife of Earl Godwin, anciently founded a conventual establishment here.

A CORNER OF OLD NAILSWORTH.   *Photo by H. J. Comley.*

THE PRIORY CHURCH, WOODCHESTER. *Photo by H. J. Comley.*

THE DOMINICAN PRIORY, WOODCHESTER. *Photo by H. J. Comley.*

Stroud as an Educational Centre.

THE publisher, in drawing attention to the various educational establishments here represented, desires to point out that the various notices of Schools are arranged in order as received, and their position in the list has no connection with their relative importance, which must be judged by the reader.

Stratford Abbey College.

STRATFORD Abbey College is an elegant and commodious family mansion, standing in its own grounds, just outside Stroud, and specially adapted for a School.

The Schoolrooms are fitted with modern arrangements; there are eight separate Music Rooms and a large Studio for Drawing and Painting. The sanitary arrangements and ventilation are throughout according to the most recent improvements, and the neighbourhood is well known as a health resort. The playground is fitted with swings, see-saws and trapese. A large garden is attached, with meadow, tennis lawn, cricket and hockey grounds. There is also a Gymnasium.

Miss ISACKE, the Principal, who is a Queen's Medallist and an Academic Member of Trinity College, has had much experience in education, and can offer the highest testimonials from parents of former pupils. References will be exchanged if required.

All the comforts of a Christian home are afforded, with the privileges and refinements of a family. Healthful, moral and religious training, high mental culture, with self-government, and habits of industry are the chief points aimed at.

A portion of time is devoted to Plain and Ornamental Needlework. Pupils are not required to commit to memory lessons they do not understand, nor to learn unexplained rules.

Particular attention is bestowed on the formation of Christian principles, and on mental culture and bodily development.

DISCIPLINE.—The discipline of the College is firm but kind, its object being to prevent as well as to correct faults. A list of School Rules is placed in every room, in order that no pupil may be ignorant of the regulations necessarily adopted to ensure reasonable discipline. The pupils take daily walks with the Governesses.

THE SCHOOL COURSE includes Religious Instruction, Reading, Writing, the English Language, Literature and Composition, Elocution, Latin, Modern Languages, History, Geography, Arithmetic, Mathematics, Political Economy, Natural Science, Drawing in every style, Oil and Water Colour Painting from Life and Still Life, Singing, Voice Training, Theory of Music, Harmony, Counterpoint, Dancing, Musical Drill and Needlework (Plain and Fancy).

THE REPORT of all School work of each pupil is sent to the Parents or Guardian three times a year, also weekly cards showing position and marks; and special care is bestowed on backward and delicate pupils.

A SANATORIUM is situated close to the School, with Resident Nurse.

Parents are requested to send for an illustrated Souvenir of Stratford Abbey College, with references, etc., sent post-free on application.

STRATFORD ABBEY COLLEGE.   (See page 120.)

STRATFORD ABBEY COLLEGE—THE GARDEN. (See page 120.)

Stroud Ladies' College,

Beeches Green, Stroud, Gloucestershire.

STROUD LADIES' COLLEGE, BEECHES GREEN.

Principals : The Misses Howard.

Head Mistress, resident B.A.

Assisted by Certificated Teachers.

The pupils are prepared for the various public Examinations.

Number of Pupils limited.

The House is situated on high ground near the town.

Prospectus on application.

Abbotsford College, Stroud.

(Roxburgh House.)

BOARDING AND DAY SCHOOL FOR GIRLS.

ABBOTSFORD COLLEGE, STROUD.

Principal : Miss Cranstoun, who is assisted by resident English and Foreign Governesses and Visiting Masters.

The house stands within its own grounds and occupies one of the best sites in Stroud.

The Course of Instruction includes thorough English, French, German, Latin, Mathematics, Science, Drawing, Painting, Theory of Music, Class-Singing, Needlework, Calisthenics, etc.

Private Lessons are given in French, German, Piano, Violin, Solo Singing, etc., and Special Classes are arranged for Elocution, Gymnastics, and Dancing.

Pupils are prepared for the London Matriculation, Oxford and Cambridge Local, Associated Board (R.A.M. and R.C.M.), Trinity College, London, and South Kensington Examinations.

Prospectus, references, and full particulars on application.

The High School for Girls, Stroud.

Principals :

Miss L. Kember, (University of Cambridge Higher Examination for Women, Honours and Distinctions).

Miss F. Kember, (Full Art Class Teachers' Certificate, Ablett's System and South Kensington Method).

Miss M. Knee, Trained Kindergarten and Health Mistress.

The School Course includes Scripture Knowledge, thorough English, Mathematics, Latin, French, German, Botany, Physiology and Hygiene, Geology and Physical Geography, Drawing, Modelling, Swedish Drill, Theory of Music, Class Singing and Needlework.

School Examinations are held at the end of each term and Reports upon the progress and attendance of pupils sent to the parents. Pupils are prepared for the University Locals. Preparatory Department for Boys and Girls, with Kindergarten Training.

Boys are also prepared for the Entrance Examinations to Schools or Colleges.

The School Year is divided into Three Terms of about Thirteen weeks each.

Lessons in Music, Special Drawing and Painting Lessons, Drill Classes.

Solo Singing, Pianoforte, Violin, Advanced Drawing and Painting, Leather Work, Chip Carving and Miniature Painting on Ivory, are extra. Outside students may be admitted for these subjects.

Pupils prepared for the Science and Art Examinations, South Kensington, and for the Art Class Teachers' Certificate, also for the Associated Board of the Royal Academy and Royal College of Music, for the Incorporated Society of Musicians, and for the Trinity College, London.

Visiting Music Mistress, Mrs. Turner, A.R.C.O.

The Hygienic arrangements have been examined and approved by the Sanitary Inspector.

References kindly permitted to :—

The Rev. J. H. Moulton, M.A., Fellow of King's College, Cambridge, 3, Queen Anne Terrace, Cambridge.

Miss Law, L.L.A., The High School, Rotherham.

The Rev. J. Dalton, M.A., Hickleton Vicarage, Doncaster.

The Rev. E. H. Hawkins, M.A., Holy Trinity Vicarage, Stroud.

W. J. Greenstreet, Esq., M.A., Head Master, The Marling School, Stroud.

Miss Ellis, L.L.A., Principal, Oldfield Lodge School, Bath.

W. Harbutt, Esq., R.C.A., The Grange, Bathampton, Bath.

John Fisher, Esq., Kensington School of Art, Berkeley Square, Bristol.

Joseph Deeley, Esq., M.A., Fortescue House, Bedford Park, Chiswick.

Music and Photography.

One of the most interesting establishments in the town of Stroud is at 5, George Street, where visitors will find all they require in Music and Photography.

Originally established by the late Mr. T. W. Dauncey in 1849 as a music warehouse, it was acquired by the late Mr. Edgar H. Barnard some two years ago. Mr. Barnard took no part in the management of the business himself, but retained Mr. T. C. Dauncey as manager. On Mr. Barnard's death in November last, his nephew, Mr. T. Knight Barnard, succeeded to the business. Mr. T. Knight Barnard was for nine years Student and Sub-Professor at the Royal Academy of Music, and afterwards established with much success the Redhill College of Music with a staff of Professors from the R.A.M. He will now reside in the district and give the business in George Street his personal supervision, and all clients may now rely upon their enquiries and wants receiving prompt and courteous attention. None but the finest tuners and workmen are employed, and all orders will be carried out in a manner second to no other establishment in the trade.

Colour Photography.

A WONDERFUL EXHIBIT.

Visitors to 5, George Street will also find a splendid selection of Photographic Apparatus, a selection **quite novel and unique**, for it will contain examples of the latest advance in Colour Photography.

Mr. T. Knight Barnard, who is the Patentee of this invention, can show visitors examples of Colour work far ahead of anything hitherto produced, for the shimmer of burnished metal, the glitter of glass, and the delicate tints and shades of rare flowers, etc., are all reproduced with a realism which **words cannot adequately describe.**

All interested in Photography should spare a few minutes to see these wonderful photographs, and those doing so will find a most hearty welcome at 5, George Street.

Old Chapel, Stroud.

CONGREGATIONAL.

Pastor = = = = = Rev. R. M. Ross.

CHURCH FOUNDED, 1687   CHAPEL BUILT, 1711.

Renovated or Enlarged : 1813, 1828, 1844, 1873, 1881, 1898.

INTERIOR OF OLD CHAPEL.

Sunday Services   -   -   -   11 a.m. and 6-30 p-m.

Sunday School   -   -   -   10 a.m. and 2-30 p.m.

Week Evening Services: Monday, 7-30.

Christian Endeavour Society:
Wednesday—Juniors, 7 o'clock; Seniors, 8 o'clock.

VISITORS CORDIALLY WELCOMED.

Bedford Street,
Congregational Chapel,
STROUD.

Minister = = = = Rev. G. Barrett.

BEDFORD STREET CONGREGATIONAL CHAPEL, STROUD.

SUNDAY SERVICES:

Morning, 11.   Evening, 6-30,

SUNDAY SCHOOL:

Morning, 10.   Afternoon, 2-45.

MONDAY:

Christian Endeavour Society, 7-30.

TUESDAY:

Literary Society Meeting, 8 (during Winter Months).

WEDNESDAY:

Prayer Meeting - - - - - 6-45.
Pleasant Evening Service - - - 7-30,

The Baptist Church, Stroud.

JOHN STREET BAPTIST CHAPEL, STROUD.

The Baptist Church in Stroud was founded by the Rev. Henry Hawkins, of Eastcombe. The site, a piece of ground lying at the end of Kendrick's Orchard, was purchased in 1823, and the Chapel, erected at a cost of £2,000, including site, was opened July 1st, 1824. Mr. Hawkins was succeeded by his son-in-law, the Rev. William Yates, whose ministry lasted 40 years. Two of his daughters, Mrs. Wall and Miss Yates, have been for many years missionaries in Rome. The Rev. C. A. Davis, who settled in 1895, is the present minister. The chapel seats 750. The new Schoolroom in Union Street was erected in 1901, at a cost of £1,350.

JOHN STREET BAPTIST CHAPEL, STROUD—INTERIOR.

Wesleyan Church,

Castle Street, Stroud.

THE WESLEYAN CHURCH, STROUD.

SERVICES and MEETINGS.

SUNDAY—Divine Worship	- - - -	11 and 6-30.
„ School and Bible Class	- - -	10 and 2-30.
MONDAY—Classes	- - - - - -	7 p.m.
TUESDAY—Class	- - - - - -	3 p.m.
„ Divine Worship	- - - -	7-30 p.m.
WEDNESDAY—Women's Guild	- - -	3 p.m.
„ Classes	- - - - -	7 p.m.
„ Wesley Guild for Young People		8 p.m.
THURSDAY—Band of Hope	- - - -	7 p.m.
FRIDAY—Prayer Meeting	- - - - -	7-30 p.m.

MARRIAGE

is solemnized according to the new Act of 1898,
without the presence of a Registrar.

Apply to the Resident Minister.

BAPTISM

is administered at any Public Service.

THE GALLERY OF THE CHURCH IS FREE.

Frederick Steele & Co.,
Wallbridge Works, Stroud.

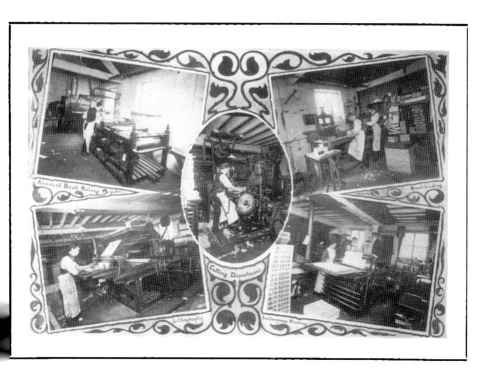

THE Views given herewith, show some of the processes carried on at the works of FREDERICK STEEL & Co., Fine Colour and General Printers, Manufacturing Stationers and Paper Agents. The leading department is the Letterpress Printing, in which branch of the trade this firm have a reputation, by no means purely local, of which they are justly proud, being more particularly marked as experts in Catalogue and Booklet production, Process and Fine Art Printing, and highest class Commercial work, for which they have laid down special plant, to which additions are frequently being made. They also have an extensive run of Colour work, both Letterpress and Lithographic; and Account Book and Pattern Card Making and Bookbinding give employment to a number of hands. The Firm have branches in Gloucester and Cheltenham. Though established but a few years, they do a considerable amount of Trade work, proving they are acknowledged in the craft itself as first-rate exponents of the printer's art.

The Imperial Hotel, Stroud.

EVERY visitor to Stroud must perforce have noticed the "Imperial Hotel," which, covered with climbing plants, occupies the space immediately facing the Great Western Station.

The "Imperial" has been so long associated with Stroud that it has well-nigh the importance of one of its public buildings, and in Mr. J. Libby's "Twenty Years' Recollections of Stroud, 1870-1890," appears the following :— "The façade of the Imperial Hotel is very imposing, and its internal arrangements and decorations are a credit to the town. Mrs. Lawson carries on the business of the hotel, and it is one of the most comfortable and well-conducted in the West of England."

THE IMPERIAL HOTEL. *Photo by H. J. Comley.*

Visitors will find at this modern hotel every comfort and convenience.

There are several suites of Private Rooms. The Public Rooms include large Coffee Room (with separate tables), Commercial Room, Lounge and Smoking Room, Billiard Room, Stock Rooms, etc.

Visitors are catered for by the week, month or year. Although centrally situated, there is a very fine view from the windows of the "Imperial."

Posting in all its branches. Covered Yard and good Loose Boxes.

Terms on application to Mrs. Lawson, The Imperial Hotel, Stroud.

CAINSCROSS BREWERY.

NOT the least interesting feature in the immediate vicinity of Stroud is the above well-known landmark seen from the Great Western Railway or the Cainscross Road, as one approaches the town from Gloucester.

The name of the firm "CARPENTER & Co." is a synonym for delicate high-class Pale Ales, in the production of which purity and excellence are the chief watch-words.

From small beginnings this brewery has been built up into the well-equipped and up-to-date establishment, which to-day invites inspection, and its steady development, with the increasing hold it has obtained on all classes in the neighbourhood, evinces the fact that the Public still show their discriminating taste in the matter of the National beverage. It is one of the very few remaining

breweries which make the Family trade the first consideration. No intelligent observer can go over it without perceiving that the Firm aim to keep in the very front of their profession, and that the public taste which has so rapidly developed a preference for wholesome, light and sound Ales is here successfully met.

The Cainscross Brewery has exceptional advantages in its valuable water supply, derived from two deep springs. One of them, brought from a distant hillside, pours a continuous crystal stream into a tank at the top of the brewery. This being of exceptional purity is used exclusively for brewing ; whilst the other, on account of its extremely low temperature, is invaluable for cooling and other purposes.

Mild and Pale Bitter Ales and Stout may be obtained in casks of all sizes, screw-stopper bottles, and jars conveniently fitted with stopper and tap.

The Firm are always pleased to show Customers and Visitors over the Brewery and Maltings.

Rodborough Court,

STROUD,

The Residence of ALFRED APPERLY, Esq., J.P.,

One of the best examples of
modern architecture in the district.

It was designed and rebuilt in 1888
by ALFRED BUCKNALL, Esq., of Clifton,

With additions in 1899 by
P. MORLEY HORDER, Esq., of London.

A View of Hyde Farm, situated between
6co and 700 feet above sea level.

Flock of Registered Hampshire Down Sheep,
at Hyde Farm, near Stroud,

The property of ALFRED APPERLY, Esq., J.P., Rodborough Court, Stroud.

Honours and prizes have been obtained at several shows during 1901 and 1902.

The Wool from this splendid flock, augmented
by purchases from other noted Breeders,
is now used in the manufacture of the celebrated

English Cloth, "Hydea,"
(REGISTERED),

(A name derived from that of the Farm
where the flock is kept).

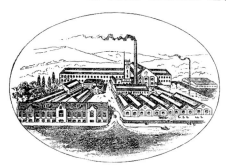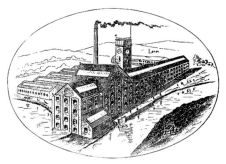

Apperly, Curtis & Co., Limited,

Dudbridge Mills, Stroud, West of England.

This business was established in 1794 by the grandfather of Mr. Alfred Apperly, the present Chairman and Managing Director of the Company. At the 1851 Exhibition, the Gold Medal for the finest cloth in the world was awarded.

The mills, which are amongst the largest in the district, are equipped with a complete electrical installation for power and lighting, and are furnished with all the latest and most up-to-date machinery for the production of high-class woollen cloths.

In the arrangement of the mills, special attention has been paid to the comfort and convenience of the workpeople, and the provision made for these has elicited the warmest approval of the Factory Act Inspectors and other Government officials.

Apperly, Curtis & Co., Ltd., is the first cloth-making firm which has made systematic and continued experiments for the purpose of utilizing English wool in the production of high-class West of England fabrics.

The results have been very successful, and highly laudatory notices of them have appeared, not only in the trade journals, but in all the leading newspapers of the English press. These draw attention to the fact that " Hydea " cloths are remarkable, not only for the fixity of their dyes, and the permanency of their colors, but also that they are thoroughly sanitary fabrics, and are produced in a variety of styles to suit all classes. We need not hesitate to draw attention to other advantages incidental to the introduction upon the market of English cloth made from English wool. The best interests of our race are endangered by the increasing tendency of our agricultural labourers to migrate to the large towns. How to get our men back to the land is a serious problem which has long been occupying the attention of our publicists and statesmen. Should the attempt to introduce an English cloth of English wool be successful, there is but little doubt that it will be widely imitated. In that case the English farmer will soon be able to command such a price for his wool that the agricultural community will be largely benefited by our initiative. A great step will then have been taken to stem the tide of imigration to the large towns, which is already having such a deleterious effect on the physical development of the present generation.

That the *Times* and other newspapers are justified in their encomiums of the cloth itself, and of the idea of producing English cloth of English Wool, is proved by the fact that " Hydea " cloth having been introduced to the notice of the King, His Majesty has been graciously pleased to command that a piece be forwarded to Sandringham.

Thus it will be seen that even in these times enlightened enterprise has its reward, and by such enterprise it is satisfactory to note that the fame of the West of England as a centre of high-class cloth production is deservedly maintained.

J. Garnick,

Tailor & Breeches Maker.

FOR several years J. GARNICK has made a lead of First-class RIDING BREECHES. The constantly increasing area of his connection is sufficient proof that Cheltenham is not too distant from anywhere for a thoroughly reliable pair of Breeches.

West of England, Scotch, and all kinds of materials for Gentlemen's and Ladies' Tailoring.

The "Hydea" Tweed, made from Wool grown on the backs of English Sheep.

ADDRESS—1, Portland Street and 1, Albion Street, CHELTENHAM.

GLOUCESTER CATHEDRAL.   (12 miles from Stroud.)

Stroud Provident Benefit Building Society.

Established 1850.
Incorporated 1877.

Accumulated Permanent Guarantee Fund, £7,250.

THE Reduced Scale of Monthly Repayments, calculated at 4 per cent. interest (with annual rests), enables Borrowers to purchase the Houses they occupy for about the same amount they pay in rent, thus converting their payments into a **Permanent Investment** for themselves and families.

Advances are made upon Houses or Land, repayable by Monthly Instalments. This offers great facility to Borrowers to purchase Property, to **Build their own Houses,** or to redeem existing Mortgages. The Mortgage cannot be called in if the Monthly instalments are kept up.

No Charge is made to the Borrower for Mortgage Deed.

INVESTORS' DEPARTMENT.

Investment Shares are payable by Monthly Subscriptions of from 1/8 to 10/- for a single share. A new feature is the introduction of Short Period Shares.

Shares may now be taken for the following terms—

Class **D**	....	Realizable in 4 years and 8 months.
Class **C**	....	Realizable in 8 years and 7 months.
Class **B**	....	Realizable in 14 years and 6 months.

Prospectus with full information from the Chief Office.

Secretary : –G. F. PAYNE.   Solicitors :—WINTERBOTHAM & SONS.

Head Office :—5, Rowcroft, Stroud.

140

141

GODSELL & SONS

TRADE MARK.

PALE ALE and STOUT BREWERS.

An excellent **LIGHT DINNER ALE (AK)**, at 1/= per gallon, brewed specially for the private family trade.

NOURISHING STOUT, at 1/4 per gallon.

Salmon's Spring Brewery, STROUD.

Branches—CHELTENHAM: 4, Regent Street;
GLOUCESTER: The Cross, 47, Eastgate Street.

T. E. Revell & Son,

FAMILY BOOTMAKERS,

67, High Street, STROUD,

and 6, Bridge Street, Bath.

Real Hygienic Boots and Shoes made strictly to the normal shape
of the feet, as recommended by the Medical Faculty.

Well-cut Leggings of the newest patterns.
Athletic Boots and Shoes of all descriptions.
Hunting and Coachmen's Top Boots to measure.

Orders per Post or Telephone receive prompt attention.

Established 1871.   TELEPHONE No. 148 Y 4.

THE STROUD SHOWROOM of ..

Truscott & Son, Limited.

Harness

Pair-Horse
and Single,
Best London
Style and
Finish.

AGENT for

**Fleming's
Registered
Hoof
Dressing
and Horse
Ointments.**

ESTABLISHED
1845.

**Every
Requisite
for Horse
and Stable.**

A. H. SARGEANT,
15, KING STREET, STROUD.

The Old-established and Up-to-date
Saddler and Harness Maker, . . .

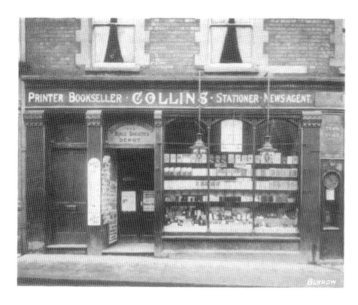

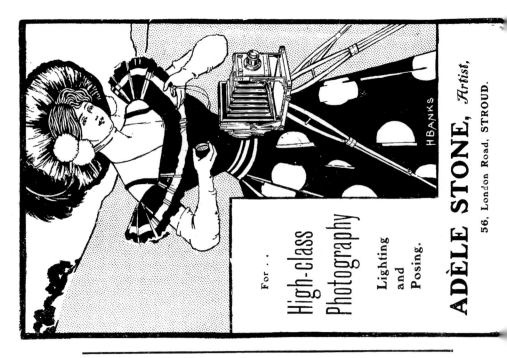

For ..
High-class
Photography

Lighting
and
Posing.

ADÈLE STONE, *Artist,*

56, London Road, STROUD.

H BANKS

WALTER GUILDING,

⤳ *Pastry Cook and Confectioner,*

FancyBread
and Biscuit
Maker,

33,
High St.
(Near the
Cross),
Stroud.

Bride Cakes
Creams and
Jellies,
a Speciality

Crumpets and all kinds of Buns, Cakes and Contectionery
made to order. *School and Private Tea Parties supplied.*

The Verlands

(Late the Old Vicarage),

Painswick,

Gloucestershire.

Under the personal management
of the Proprietors—

Mr. & Mrs. Russell.

Premises now being enlarged, Seven more Bedrooms
being added in consequence of great demand.

Superior Board

Residence.

Per Week, or Special
for long periods.

Tariff on Application.

THE VERLANDS is beautifully situated on the Cotswold Hills at Painswick; is high and bracing; commanding lovely views of the surrounding country; pronounced by visitors to nearly equal anything of the sort in England; has charming Lawns and Gardens; shady walks; Tennis and Croquet.

Golf Links quite near.

Close to Church and Post Office.
Bath Room (hot and cold).

Sanitation and Water perfect.
Every Home Comfort.

Post and Telegraph Office : Painswick.
Station : Stroud (Midland and G.W.R.) $3\frac{1}{2}$ miles.

F. E. SLADE, GROCER AND COAL MERCHANT, GENERAL STORES, EBLEY.

Best Household COALS delivered to all parts of the District.

J. W. SMITH, *Hairdresser, Wig Maker and Perfumer, ...*

Established 1820. **7, King Street, STROUD,**

Respectfully Solicits your Patronage.

Combs and Brushes.   *Toilet and Bath Sponges.*   *Standard Perfumery.*

George Birt,

Family Grocer and Provision Merchant.

❧❧❧

BRITISH AND FOREIGN WINES.

Agent for...

Kola, Kande, Mazawattee, Tower and other Teas.

DRINK, ENJOY and ... RECOMMEND **BIRT'S 1/6 and 2/- TEAS.**

Fresh Arrivals of Wiltshire Butter Every Wednesday and Friday.

Finest Canadian Cheese, Wiltshire Bacon, New Zealand Butter, all at the Lowest Market Prices.

4 & 5, High Street, STROUD.

Ward Waterman

Ladies' and - - -
Gentlemen's Tailor,

LANSDOWN, STROUD.

BEST - CLASS STYLE AND WORKMANSHIP
GUARANTEED.

**A Choice Selection of Materials from the Best
Makers always in Stock.**

Agent for BURBERRY YARN PROOF CLOTHS.

J. Thomas,

Dyer, Cleaner and Feather Dresser,

7, LANSDOWN, STROUD.

High-class Work,
Moderate Charges,
Despatch.

Speciality : Dry Cleaning.

Goods by Post,
Rail or Carrier
receive prompt
attention.   Estd. 1845.

The Purest Table Water from Malvern Spring.

"Burrow's"

☞ SPARKLING ☜

Malvern Water

Champagne Pints, 3/6 per dozen,

SOLD EVERYWHERE.

Burrow's is the **Only Genuine**
"ALPHA BRAND."

Ask for "Burrow's." *Telegrams, "Springs, Malvern."*
Absolutely Pure, without any
Added Ingredient.

W. & J. BURROW,

The Springs, Malvern.

For Cakes, Pastry, Buns and Confectionery

of every description,
GO TO . .

Walter Farrar,

Wholesale & Retail Confectioner, ...

Kendrick Street,
STROUD,

Where you will always
get Fresh Goods
at Lowest Possible Prices.

Tea and Coffee always ready.

A TRIAL SOLICITED.

FRANK GILL,

MANUFACTURING AND FURNISHING

IRONMONGER,

STROUD. Telephone 149X.

MILL FURNISHER.

Kitchen Ranges
and Tile Registers.

Lawn Mowers, Rollers and
Garden Requisites.

BRUSHES, DOOR MATS, Etc.   BEST SHEFFIELD CUTLERY.

Lamps, Oil, Tool and Paint Merchant.

CARTRIDGES AND SPORTING AMMUNITION.

Stone's

Restaurant
and..
Refreshment
Rooms,

9, GLOUCESTER ST.,

STROUD.

HAM and BEEF
of the best quality
always in cut.

Every Accommodation for Cyclists and Football Teams.

John Bryant,

*Dealer in Antique Furniture,
China, Clocks, Etc.,*

George
Street,
Stroud,
Glos.

Established
1857.

C. J. DAUNCEY,

Hosier, Hatter and Outfitter,

1 and 2, Bridge Street, NAILSWORTH, Glos.

The Noted House for..

'Ardwear' Boots and Shoes.

New Crown Strap Leggings and Gaiters,

Fox's New Patent PUTTEES.

❋

Jaeger Pure Wool Underwear.

Agent for the celebrated

Cellular Clothing.

❋

The Newest and Up-to-date Novelties in

Men's, Youths', Boys' and Juvenile Wear.

❋

BRITISH SPORTS.

Cricket, Lawn Tennis, Golf, Football, Hockey, Gymnasia, and all..

Outdoor and Indoor Games.

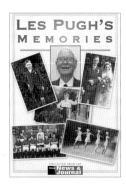

Les Pugh's Memories

LES PUGH

Les Pugh is well known in the Stroud area for his absorbing memories that have appeared over the years in the *Stroud News & Journal*. Recalling life from the early 1900s, these columns have now been collated into this fascinating book giving a glimpse of a life few now remember. Les has seen a great many changes during his lifetime and with his rare gift for recollecting intricate details from the past and the clarity of writing, the reader will be absorbed by poignant memories of those far-off days.

978 0 7524 4791 9

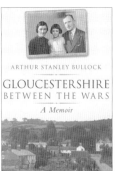

Gloucestershire Between the Wars

A.S. BULLOCK

One of the most eventful periods in history – the first half of the twentieth century – is vividly and astutely described by A.S. Bullock in this entertaining memoir. Arthur grew up in Longhope in the Forest of Dean and after his service in the First World War and his struggle to find employment in Birmingham and South Wales, he worked at Lister's in Dursley. From there he moved to Stroud and set up a business at Port Mills, Brimscombe, just before the onset of the Second World War.

978 0 7524 4793 3

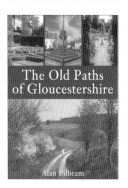

The Old Paths of Gloucestershire

ALAN PILBEAM

In this fascinating account, Alan Pilbeam takes us on a tour of the county's pathways and roads, demonstrating how the evolution of Gloucestershire society over time, from the pilgrims of the Middle Ages through the battle-scars of the Civil War and the industrial workers of the Victoria era, is reflected in both the uses and nature of the county's footpaths. Yet, this is more than simply a history book and will hold appeal not only to walkers, but to anyone with an interest in the history of the county.

978 0 7524 4540 3

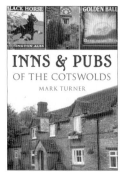

Inns & Pubs of the Cotswolds

MARK TURNER

This A-Z covering Gloucestershire, Oxfordshire, Warwickshire and Worcestershire is a delightful tour around the most interesting pubs in the area. Taking in all manner of establishments such as the Coach & Horses, an old village pub in Longborough, to the White Hart Royal Hotel, a sixteenth-century inn in Moreton-on-Marsh, the author visits a huge variety of inns and pubs that have made the Cotswolds the delightful area they are today.

978 0 7524 4465 9

If you are interested in purchasing other books published by The History Press, or in case you have difficulty finding any History Press books in your local bookshop, you can also place orders directly through our website
www.thehistorypress.co.uk